Off the Beat

Off the Beat

by
Maureen O'Toole

HODDER AND STOUGHTON

Printed in Great Britain for Hodder and Stoughton Limited
St. Paul's House, Warwick Lane, London, E.C.4
by Ebenezer Baylis & Son, Ltd., The Trinity Press,
Worcester, and London

Preface

by

LORD LONGFORD

It is a real privilege to write an introduction to Maureen's book. Maureen O'Toole is not her real name and the names of almost all the other characters have been altered to avoid causing distress to anyone.

There seemed to me three reasons why this book should be of value. First, it is a vivid human story, told in her own words by the principal figure. She has had generous professional help in re-arranging her material, but she had completed a first draft of the book on her own, some of it written before she retired from her profession. To those who wonder whether some of the descriptions are too lurid to appear in print. I can only say that Maureen has been most anxious to avoid shocking anyone unnecessarily — as will be noticed in more than one passage, she has deliberately omitted extreme details.

Secondly, her story should be full of instruction for social workers of many kinds, who so often feel themselves at a loss to understand what leads girls like Maureen to embark on such a life. There are not a few examples within these pages of well-intentioned efforts to help which went astray. Parents also, mothers most obviously, and for that matter brothers and sisters, can find much to ponder here. Maureen was, on her own showing, a naughty child who became increasingly more naughty under the treatment meted out to her at home and in various schools. Gradually, naughtiness led her further and further into delinquency and vice. Not only families but all who teach the young may well ask themselves how many now in their care are liable to tread the same path unless more affection and understanding are shown.

Finally, the religious message is clear and moving. Here at

least is one brand who was plucked from the burning. She has referred to me in terms that are far too flattering and she mentions others who have rendered her much more lasting help, including the wonderful friends with whom she is living now, but it is difficult not to feel that the grace of God has descended on her in a quite startling manner. That is obviously what she herself feels and I would think that many who read her book will agree with her.

Author's Note

I would like to thank Lord Longford, Mr. Robin Denniston and Mrs. Mary Hobbs for all the help and encouragement they have given me in preparing this book for publication.

MAUREEN O'TOOLE

Prologue

IT IS four-thirty in the morning. I can hear the milkman rattling the bottles and his torch makes a flash of light on my wall. I keep my clock fast—it is a whole hour ahead by now—but if ever I forget to wind it, I can always rely on the milkman as my time signal. I like to get up in the very early hours, nearly always before four, but then of course my day's work finishes just as early, and I try to go to sleep about seven each evening. The doctors say I need long rest to make up for the past.

So early in the morning, I have to be very quiet, for there are three or four old ladies sleeping round me—luckily they are a little hard of hearing. First of all, I pour out a cup of tea from the Thermos and light my first cigarette. In my present life, these are my greatest luxuries. I adore my cigarettes—smoke just ten a day. Of course, there are certain parts of the convent where I am not allowed to smoke: broad-minded as the sisters are, that is understandable. It would be disrespectful and upset the older members of the community.

Next, I make my bed and tidy my room—it is very small, and as it contains everything I possess in the world, it gets pretty cramped. It is warm and cosy, however, and I love it. Sometimes I think I must have a good clear-out, but somehow, I can always think of a use for everything and it never gets done. I creep along to the bathroom, wash, and brush my teeth—I always have my bath in the evening. I creep back, dress and put on my make-up—olive oil to protect my skin, chiefly, and eyebrow pencil: Sister Ursula says I don't know how to use it properly—she offered to teach me and I think she probably could! We met in the corridor last week when she came off night duty. She was in her dressing gown without her coif—she called out 'Good morning!' and whisked out of my sight quickly, but not before I saw what a lovely head of curly golden-brown hair she has. She can't be much older than I am. She trained as a nurse, and works in the old people's home along the path.

9

When I am dressed and ready I settle back to enjoy the only part of the day I can really call my own. During working hours, I am at the beck and call of everyone – which is how it should be, since that is why I am here – but the early morning is mine. I write letters to my good friends outside – I like to answer people right away. I read the papers to keep up with what is happening, and I read religious books too, and religious novels: I like those. I do my mending – and now I am writing this book, because they want me to tell you my story.

It has just flashed on me that today is my birthday, and the Feast of the Motherhood of Our Lady. That pleases me that, if I had to be born, it was on this day that it happened. No one at the convent knows it is my birthday and I shall not tell them: I know they would make me a cake and perhaps give me presents, and it's funny, but I don't want people to give me things. If anyone is to do the giving, I feel it ought to be me!

Six o'clock. I must go out now with Chippy. About a week ago, just as I was dozing off to sleep, I heard the rustle of paper under my bedroom door. It was a note from Mother Oliver to tell me that Chippy was about to go into season. (Mother Oliver brought her over from Ireland when she was only a puppy.) Mother's idea was that I should take Chippy out for her daily walk before the early Mass, so that she would not be chased by the other dogs. What I don't think Mother Oliver realises is that as a result, now it is autumn, we walk across the fields in the pitch dark! Chippy enjoys it all, but I keep myself very much on the alert, with my stick at the ready: I am terrified of being attacked by a huge rat or something.

Nevertheless, there is a wonderful feeling about going out at this hour. It is so quiet everywhere. In the distance, I can see one or two lights in the town, and I think of the men and women who must be getting up ready for the day's work and try to say a prayer for them. Still, I am relieved when the morning light begins to break through! All summer, I took Chippy out during the day down to the lake, where she loves to swim, though she looks like a big elephant in the water. She chased the wildfowl, and I was afraid for them at first, but they always managed to escape her grasp, until it came to the stage where it was not Chippy doing the chasing, but the waterfowl.

Yesterday we trudged along in thick mist and I had to be careful I did not fall into one of the deep holes she has been digging in the fields. I could not see the town lights and I got a real fright when a huge object suddenly loomed up in front of me. I thought it was a man about to attack me, but it was a large horse. He seemed as surprised as I was—he must have wondered what on earth a human being was doing in his field so early. Sister Mark, who is in charge of locking and unlocking the main convent door, said she thought I must be very brave to go out walking at such a dark hour and I said I thought so too. I would much rather be in the quiet chapel reading, as I used to be before Chippy was in season!

I don't profess to know much about dogs on heat, but there seems to be very little difference in her—she digs away still for all she is worth. On my return, Mother Oliver always asks me anxiously whether we met any gentlemen dogs, and I assure her that there is absolutely no one, let alone a dog, in sight at that hour. It seems to me that Chippy is just not interested in sex, or perhaps she has no sex appeal. I think Mother Oliver is terrified that because of my past, I may lead Chippy astray and encourage her to have fun and games! She probably feels she must keep an eye on us both, but she need not worry.

This morning it was not as dark as usual—there had been a bright moon and very little cloud. The fields and countryside were covered in the first white frost of this winter. We were not successful with our hunting—we caught neither fieldmouse nor rabbit. There is quite a growth of grass springing in our favourite field now, and I foresee difficult walking if the grass gets much longer and wetter.

I came into Mass with a small pile of letters and birthday cards sticking out of my missal, as I had just collected my post. I noticed Father Lawrence glance at them as he passed me. Later in the morning, he asked me outright if it was my birthday. I told him why I didn't want anyone to know, but he said I might have told him at any rate, and he would have said Mass specially for me. As it was, he promised me his next free Mass—there's a great honour!

Religion used to mean very little to me, in spite of my convent upbringing (or perhaps, in view of the number of them, it should be upbringings!). My chief aim, in fact, was to get away from religion. Yet now, I sometimes wish I could stay in the chapel here all day long. I seem to have been thirsty all my life for the peace of it, with the sisters so deep in their praying that you can feel

11

them lifting you up too. It would never do, I know—that peace has to be carried out into the day's work. If only I were starting my life all over again, however, what would I not do to be stable enough, good enough and educated enough to pull my weight as a Christian, to be able to go out and help those who are now what I once was.

Sometimes when I have a moment to spare I walk up through the convent grounds to the sisters' private graveyard on the hillside. There, surrounded by about twenty graves with their stone crosses, I fall on my knees in the soft mossy grass before the impressive life-size figure of Christ crucified and pray aloud—safe in the knowledge that there is no one likely to be around to hear me. I don't just pray the usual prayers—I tell Christ whatever is on my mind at the time and ask His help and presence. Then I saunter round, stopping for a few seconds at each graveside to read the name and inscription. It always amazes me what a ripe old age these sisters lived to, though they must have been just as hard-working as their present-day successors.

It wasn't easy when I first came here. I don't think the sisters had met such a difficult girl before. They knew nothing about my past and it took me some months to feel the time was ripe to tell them. They took it very well and have never let it make any difference. For my part, I had great difficulty settling down and fitting into their routine and discipline. I knew a little about nuns of course after many years in convent schools, but I found I knew much less than I thought.

Then there was the question of language. I have always been pretty careful not to use four-letter words, and I don't like to hear them from others, but somehow, even now, one word I cannot help coming out with, though only at moments of great stress, the word 'dammit'. The sisters always discreetly pretend not to have heard—their tolerance is amazing.

It must have been pretty irritating to Sister Hilary to have flowers she had tended over the years mistaken for weeds by Maureen and vigorously uprooted as soon as their little green shoots appeared. We had many trips together to the compost heap to recover precious plants I had so treated.

Sister Hilary looks after the old people's home. She must be a young middle-age, but sometimes she looks dreadfully white and tired: old people require such love and patience. Today she is holding a sale of work and we have been very busy tidying up.

Among the many things we have moved from upstairs to downstairs and outside were a large kitchen table, a wardrobe, an old-fashioned sewing machine and (don't laugh!) a bath. After many years' service it was replaced and the builders managed to escape, leaving it stuck outside the kitchen entrance for all to see. I told Sister Hilary we would have to move it away. You would expect it would have taken five men to lift it, but the pair of us somehow transported it to an old shed about a quarter of a mile away. We rolled it, turned it over and over, through the kitchen garden, up over a field and into the shed, all in the pouring rain.

I went into the convent kitchen to dry off. Sister Clotilde and I don't always see eye to eye, and in a quiet way we tell each other in no uncertain terms what we think. Sometimes it reaches the stage when I want to pick up a plate and hurl it at her, and I am quite sure she would like to do the same to me. Somehow or other we refrain, and the next time we meet we are the best of friends. Sister Clotilde is really one of the kindest, most open-hearted religious I have met. She is a wonderful cook, but oh my, is she untidy! At times there are dishes all over the place waiting to be washed up, but she will wait until she has run out of clean ones. Sometimes when I have to pass through the kitchen on some mission or other and see this state of affairs, I can't help stopping there and then to offer to wash up. She always accepts my offer, for she just hates the job, but of course when the powers that be are around, she has to be up to scratch.

She is crazy about lighted candles in front of small statues. She has made herself a little shrine in a corner of the kitchen: a lovely statue of Our Lady, two small vases of artificial flowers and two small brass candlesticks, which she lights on every feast of Our Lady. This shrine means a lot to her, for she is deeply religious.

Sometimes when I drop into the kitchen for a cup of tea on feast days, the heat from the candles is overpowering, for the windows must not be opened in case the breeze blows out the flame. This is the signal for me to start teasing her:

'You know, Sister, the Church doesn't approve of this sort of thing, candles, flowers, statues. It's all out, Sister. Not that it's ever seemed to me the way to God—I prefer to find Him in my fellow creatures . . .' And so on, and so on, until I see she is getting so annoyed I had better call a halt.

Once I caught a little mouse which had been raiding her larder. Standing just behind her, I said, 'Sister, look! I have a nice present for you.' I knew full well what would happen. She turned and saw the mouse on my outstretched palm and jumped back with a great shriek of horror, calling out 'Maureen! Take it away. Quick!' But when I came back, she laughed as much as I did.

I know I am a bit of a tease sometimes. In fact, sometimes I say and do things just to see if I can shock the sisters, but it is amazing how unshockable they are. They know and understand far more than one thinks about what goes on outside the convent.

To go back to Sister Hilary and her sale of work. Apart from the posters announcing the date and place, it seemed to me she had made no preparations for it whatsoever. When I said so to her, she just laughed and said she was sure the good Lord would look after it for her. I think I had better keep my fingers crossed as well and not leave it all to the good Lord to see that she will at least meet her expenses, let alone make some money towards the convent's many needs. I for one want a lawn-mower which really cuts grass. For the last three years my back has ached from pushing the ancient apology for a lawn-mower which is all they possess.

I scrubbed and cleaned a dozen of the nursery tables in readiness — not that they were what you could call dirty: Sister Barbara, who is in charge of the little school up the hill, is so very tidy in her ways, and particular. Every Saturday I have to clean the school. I sweep and wash all the floors with a mop and plenty of Jeyes' fluid — I am a great believer in that, but Sister Barbara tells me to go carefully with it. Somehow, I don't think she likes the smell. I wash all the tables and chairs, put clean linen in the cots, take the soiled linen over to the convent laundry, burn the rubbish and open the windows as wide as possible to let in the fresh air.

Officially, of course, I have nothing to do with the children themselves, but sometimes Sister Barbara, when she sees me pass the window, will call me in for something and immediately the children all cry out 'Sing for us, Maureen!' So I sing the song I always give them:

> 'There was an old man called Michael Finnegan,
> He grew whiskers on his chinnegan.
> The wind came out and blew them innegan,
> Poor old Michael Finnegan. Beginnegan.'

As I sing, I dance around, and when it is finished they call out, 'More! More! More!'

14

They all adore Sister Barbara. She is a fine, big, pleasant woman, with the bloom of the countryside on her cheeks. Her own mother died when she was a young girl and she had to care for a large family of brothers and sisters, so she knows most of what there is to know about children.

· · ·

The sale of work fetched about forty pounds. That is pretty good, considering what a wet windy afternoon it was. There was only a handful of people — you can't blame the others for not venturing outside their homes. It's amazing what loyal friends the convent has, to rally round on such occasions. Sister Hilary was quite triumphant that she had proved me wrong in the matter of Our Lord.

When I was clearing up afterwards in the conservatory, I found a table of plants I knew belonged to Sister Hilary with a note on them saying 'Sold to Sister Barbara.' I asked Sister Barbara if she had bought them and she said she had, from one of the lady-helpers at the sale, for five and sixpence. I thought I had better ask Sister Hilary before I carried them up to the school. She was dumbfounded. Of course they were her plants, she said, and she had never put them into the sale. I pointed out that Sister Barbara had given five and sixpence for them, so that if she wanted them back she had better return the money. Sister Hilary refused roundly: she said Sister Barbara ought to have had more sense — she ought to have known that Sister Hilary would never sell her houseplants! So there at the moment the matter rests. They will just have to sort it out between them. I'm tired.

· · ·

And now it is Sunday. It was quite an effort to get out of bed this morning after yesterday, but I wouldn't miss Mass. Father Lawrence's sermon today was on love, the love of Christ. That is the basis of every sermon I have ever heard him preach. They are not clever sermons, coming just from the lips, but simple and right from the heart. His advice and guidance have been a great help to me here — he is so very straight.

Perhaps it seems an awful thing to say, but apart from Mass I find Sundays rather dull. To begin with, I dislike dressing up — I much prefer the jeans and pullovers which are my everyday wear, and I hate having to make myself presentable, though I suppose it is only polite to God. It is a lazy sort of day for me. After breakfast I went into the kitchen of the old folks' home and peeled some potatoes for Sister Ursula, who gave me a good cup of coffee and a biscuit. Then I went up to my room and read the Sunday newspapers. I cleaned a few pairs of shoes—I'm very fussy over clean shoes. When the Angelus rang, I went over to the convent kitchen to give Sister Clotilde a hand with the washing-up.

I had my dinner—I eat in a corner of the kitchen because, of course, I cannot have my meals with the community, as I am not one of them. I sit by the wide window, and as I am a quick eater, I can get up from the table as soon as it pleases me.

In the afternoon I took Chippy for a walk through the convent grounds to the lake. There was a faint mist in the air but the sun was trying hard to break through. I stood by the water's edge—the whole countryside was still except for the birds: waterfowl, wild geese and a large flock of seagulls who had travelled in from the coast, and flapped their wings madly in the water, raising a great spray and calling away to each other in weird shrieks. The great stillness around seemed reflected in my own body. It was possessed by a wonderful peace and stability such as I had never known: I was released even from thinking.

I am a great one for wanting just to sit back and think, and I feel it is particularly bad for me now, since before I know it, my thoughts tend to slip back to the past. The things that once happened to me are so vivid, so stamped on my memory that they are never blotted out, no matter how hard I try.

I

I WAS born in Dublin county, the youngest of a family of eight. They christened me Maureen — it means 'bitter' in the Irish. My mother was most unwilling to bear another child. She was in her late forties, her health was poor, and her hands were full coping with seven other children and a husband very much addicted to the whisky bottle.

Of my father I remember little. He died from a heart attack when I was only five. This much I will say for him — his drinking and his alcoholic outbursts were mostly in his own home. One part of the day, he would have me sitting on his knee, singing me old lullabies, dishing out sweets and biscuits and letting me lick the dregs of his glass; the next, he would be beating me with a long thin cane across my bare legs or arms.

Of course there must have been cause for this. For instance, at the bottom of the garden there was a very large old chestnut tree which was sheer delight to me to climb — partly because if I went high enough I could see into the next-door garden. My father had forbidden me this tree, but I went on climbing. He would creep softly and quietly behind me and with outstretched arm grab me by the hair of my head and lift me back onto the grass. It was very painful, but it did no good, of course — as soon as his back was turned, I would be back at the chestnut tree.

The house was quite large. We youngsters had the top as our nursery floor, with its large rooms and wide windows looking down onto acres of green fields, and in the distance the outline of the city, with its many old churches and steeples. When I was born, my mother was very ill. She kept to her own quarters until I was about three, and I was left to housemaids and nursemaids, country girls with little or no training in the upbringing of children.

I suppose I was what is called 'a beautiful baby'. They tell me that when I was wheeled out in my pram, people would stop to stare at my rosy cheeks, dark curly hair, and my large blue eyes flashing from under long black lashes. Until I was three, I was in fact a very normal child, but then something happened which, according to my family, seemed to change me completely. I developed a mastoid in my left ear. The doctor was one of the old-fashioned country type: his treatment was simply scalding-hot bread-poultices. I can remember the feeling of nakedness when they shaved away all my hair – in my mind this period stands out as one long scream.

I recovered, and when I was four, I was sent to a little nursery school. It was run by a Mrs. Coggan, who had a small dumpy body and a flaming mop of red hair. She looked after about twenty tots in one room, and it was not unusual for her to stop in the middle of the ABC to rush down to the kitchen because the stew was boiling over. We paid five shillings a week, and she called the roll from a kind of cheque book, no doubt to keep her accounts straight. Her own babies would share the room with us, and if they screamed she would undo her blouse, to our fascination, and feed them while she continued our lesson unconcerned.

My mother had married twice. Her first was what is known as an 'arranged' marriage, a wealthy one, and by it she had one daughter, whose father died when she was about seven. My mother's second marriage she called a love-match. She was a religious woman, going to Mass daily, and making sure her children observed strictly the obligations of our Roman Catholic faith. She was a great one for the praying, and as I grew older and naughtier, I would find she had sewn medals into hidden places of my clothes, no doubt hoping they would influence me for good – I spent a lot of time cutting them out! She worked hard for the church, organising whist drives and dances to raise money. She was tall, slim and elegant, and even when money was short, her clothes and shoes were hand-made and of the best. She was strict in her way too, but nothing like as strict as Father.

After his death, she found me too much to manage on her own. She took me away from Mrs. Coggan's to put me in some sort of residential home or school, and, of all places, she chose an orphanage, run by an order of nuns. It was like something out of Oliver Twist. It was a forbidding building without and within. It stood in a poor quarter of Dublin, and most of the children came from poverty-stricken families. I felt entirely alone.

At night, I would lie listening to the footsteps passing in the street below our window, and dream it would turn out that there had been some mistake when I was born, and those footsteps were my real father or mother hurrying to take me back to a loving home I would never again leave. Then I would sob myself to sleep—and each night I would wet my bed.

The sister on early morning duty always came into the small room I had to share with another bed-wetter as a punishment, to check our beds. Mine was always wet, and I was always caned. As at home, it was good and hard. It was usually carried out in front of the other children, and sometimes, to shame me more, I was ordered to take my wet mattress and sheets down to the main corridor and there kneel beside them for an hour in full view of whoever passed that way. However hard I tried, I could not stop this wetting, not only of my night but also of my day clothes. I was in my teens before I knew the comfort of wearing a dry pair of knickers.

There was another humiliating experience that all the orphanage children had to endure. Every Saturday morning when we got up, we would strip the beds and fold all the blankets, putting them neatly at the end of the bed. Then after breakfast we went back to our dormitories and each of us filled a small basin with water and placed it on a chair beside our bed. You may wonder what this was in aid of—just wait and I will tell you. We would then open our blankets and for the next hour we would carefully and slowly pick out the little brown hopping fleas. At first I found it very difficult to spot them, for they were deep in the wool of the blankets and one needed long nimble fingers to dig them out. After a few sessions, however, I became quite expert at it and in in the course of the hour sometimes made a record catch of thirty or so. The nun who supervised us allowed no talking or laughing —this was a serious business which needed all our concentration. They were a hard set of nuns, much too strict for such small children—remember, I was then not yet six.

The long dark winter nights were the hardest to bear, longing for home and dreading the morning's caning. Another punishment I had to suffer for this unfortunate bed-wetting habit of mine was to be deprived of my nightly mug of cocoa. It was thick and unsweetened, but the food was not very plentiful, and that cocoa I had to forgo left a void in my stomach, for I had always been a very hungry child.

Each week one of my brothers or sisters, but never my mother, came to visit me, and to do them justice, I think the visits were as distressing to them as they were to me. Once, early on, one brother to whom I had complained of hunger brought me an apple pie. Any such presents were supposed to be handed to the sister-in-charge and divided between all the children, and I was determined *that* should not happen. I stuffed that apple pie into my mouth so fast that I made myself sick, there in the main hall in the sight of all the visitors. I was made to go and fetch a pail and cloth, and mop up the revolting mess in front of pairs and pairs of accusing eyes.

I was at that orphanage only three months, but it felt like as many years. The day my sister came to fetch me home I was so overjoyed I cried. While the nuns read my mother's note asking for me, my sister took me on her lap—and that was doubly kind of her since my knickers were, as usual, wet!

I was sent back to a day-school, a national one, but I was very restless. At times I pined to be out in the fresh air, the open spaces, among the flowers, the birds, the wild animals. I wanted to feel the sun and the wind. I would slip out of the classroom on some excuse or other and run and run until I reached the open fields and the river. I was not particularly bright at my lessons. I liked English, history and geography, but I was hopeless at mathematics.

I must have gone to a good round dozen of schools, and from all of them, I was either expelled or taken away. The one in which I spent the longest period was an expensive convent boarding-school for young ladies, where all my sisters had been. They were all excellent pupils, and I imagine it was for that reason alone that the school kept me so long. It was a first-class up-to-date school, with large acres of parkland round it. The gardens were wonderful—an abundance of flowers, lawns in perfect condition, neat pathways and a lake with a waterfall. We were only allowed into them on Church feast-days, however. There were also playing-fields for hockey and cricket, and tennis courts.

They took me at a younger age than was usual because of my sisters, and when I first began attending, there were still some strange customs which were later done away with. When we took our baths, for instance, we had to wear long white cotton shifts when we climbed in, and somehow contrive to wash ourselves under them without exposing an inch of our naked bodies to the view!

The long summer evenings there seemed to me designed to give me longer for mischief. I would creep into the school orchard and fill my knickers with apples which I had not given time to get ripe. I shared them out among my friends, and the breaking into the orchard was itself a mild matter compared with the agonies I underwent during prep. All the juniors and seniors, some hundred of us, were gathered together in the hall under the supervision of one of the teaching nuns. All would be quiet, then I would see one of my friends open her desk, hide her head beneath it and crash! —at least, that is what it sounded like to me—there would be the hard crunch of a juicy apple. I would hold my breath, waiting for the whole escapade to be brought to light: I never could understand why they would not be more careful where they chose to eat their apples.

After some weeks, when the apples were becoming larger, rounder and riper, I became tired of doing all the dirty work, and managed to persuade five other girls to come with me. For fourteen glorious days we made these raids, then the head gardener went to Reverend Mother. She felt sure the thefts must be the work of the boys from the nearby preparatory school. They were questioned by their headmaster and were most indignant: they volunteered the information they had spotted some of the young ladies from the convent school entering the orchard. There was nothing for it but to own up.

The following Sunday morning after Mass, the whole school was assembled in the hall. One by one our names were called out and we had to walk the length of the hall to receive five strokes of the cane on the open hand. We were also to be fined two pounds each to pay for the wire-netting damaged. My name was the last to be called and I was about to come forward when Reverend Mother's voice broke into the silence: 'There is no need for you to come further, Maureen. I have decided you are just not worth the punishing.'

It was the worst form of punishment she could have inflicted on me, there in front of the whole school. I have never forgotten my feeling of despair and hopelessness. I was not a reformed character after that, however—far from it! I remember how the chapel fascinated me: when it was quite silent and empty after the nuns had finished their Office, I would creep in and up to their choirstalls. There, holding my breath for fear at my daring, I would go through their books taking out the brightly coloured holy pictures they were using as markers.

Religion played a very important part in our education at that school. On the first Sunday in every month, we had Exposition of the Blessed Sacrament, and we all had to take part in the Watch after Mass. This meant that in all we spent two or three hours in chapel, a long time for the smaller children, kneeling upright, with the smell of the incense and the heat from the candles overpowering you.

Every year we also had a three-day retreat. The frequent sermons were a bit dull, but I looked forward to being able to walk round the grounds in the open air in silence reading religious books, and I enjoyed making my confession no end – I used to invent amazing sexual escapades with boys to see if I could shock some information out of the priest in return – I never got very much, but occasionally they would rise to the bait.

Even though for a long period of my life I gave up going to confession, because I had no intention of changing my way of life, I have never been frightened of that sacrament. I think it is because my first experience was a happy one. I was only six when I took it into my head I must be like the rest of my family and go into the confessional. I did not say it was my first confession and I was asked how long since the last. To which I replied, 'About a hundred and fifty years!' The startled priest took a good look at me, gave me some kindly words of advice and sent me home with a bunch of holy pictures.

I have always been at home in churches, even when I was small, and familiarity led me into such escapades as taking out all the candles for sale and setting them up on the stand and lighting them to see the wonderful blaze.

When I was at that school the yo-yo craze was sweeping the country. Every girl in the Junior School had one. I was fascinated by them and took a quick spin every moment I could find – needless to say, my yo-yo spent much of its time in the teacher's desk. One morning I was sent on an errand to the Staff Room. No one was there, and idly I picked up the local newspaper. In it was an announcement of a yo-yo demonstration to be held in a big city store that very day, followed by a children's competition, with a brand new yo-yo for the champion. I determined that would be me.

During maths, I put up my hand and asked to leave the room – I had told none of my friends of my plan. It was all dead easy: no one was about. I picked up my hat and blazer and made my getaway. I had just enough money in my pocket for the fare into town. I soon found myself on the store's platform, showing the judges just how good my backward-, forward- and upward-spins were. They thought them good too and gave me the yo-yo. I stepped down and stood admiring my prize.

There was a sharp tap on my shoulder: I swung round hastily to face—my mother! When the school discovered I was missing, Reverend Mother had phoned her, and with the sixth sense some mothers have, Mother had guessed just where I would be. Containing her anger, she handed me my bus-fare and told me to return as fast as I could. I was to tell no one I had seen her: she was terrified that, if the truth came out, I would be expelled at last.

It was nearly dusk when I arrived, and all the doors that I tried, door after door, seemed locked. In a panic, I was about to try the chapel door when it was opened by Reverend Mother. I was expecting the worst, but she spoke in a very kind voice and seemed concerned only about my safety. I told her I had been roaming all these hours over the parkland, and she seemed to believe me, and taking me by the arm escorted me to the dining room and arranged for a meal to be brought. She told me gently not to worry, that all was well. It was more than I deserved—no caning, and a brand new yo-yo in my pocket.

The other girls were full of envy and praised my daring when I told them what I had really done. They were still talking of it at bedtime and I was pretty proud of myself and very restless. The junior dormitory was fairly large; it slept about thirty in single cubicles along the two walls. At one end of the lines slept a nun and many a time, lying in my bed just after lights-out, I would watch the candlelight shadows coming from her cubicle dancing on the wall as she undressed and went to bed. It passed the time before sleep caught up with me. Once we had said our night prayers, we were supposed to keep strict silence until next morning, but we were always whispering and planning pranks.

The evening of the yo-yo incident, I went up to the dormitory before anyone else and tied a small hand-bell to the spring under the nun's bed. I told the others what I had done and they were delighted. There was a great rush to get bathed and into bed, ready for the fireworks.

All was silence. Sister was undressing, the shadows were dancing up and down the wall. The candle was extinguished, she plopped onto her bed—and the hand-bell rang madly. We roared with laughter, but it was short-lived. I was called from my bed and wrapped in my dressing gown and ordered to kneel in the dark for one hour outside Sister's cubicle, without even the comfort of the dancing shadows.

Holiday times would come — I loved the summer most of all, when once again I could run free. Most of the time we spent by the sea, but sometimes we stayed with an uncle and aunt in the country. Their home stood in a hundred acres of land — the drive up to it was two miles long — and I loved to go there, in the lovely Galway countryside. The house was old and rambling, and had its own private chapel, which had seen many a priest on the run in the penal times, although now it was little used.

Aunt Maire was kind and soft-spoken and devoted to her husband and children. She was domesticated and capable as only a farmer's wife can be, and they had three girls and two boys. Uncle Sean was my father's brother and, like him, was addicted to the alcohol. Some evenings, when Auntie knew that he had gone to a big market meeting at a nearby town, she would pack us all off to bed early before his return, as she had a pretty good idea what state he would be in. Naturally this made me the more curious, and once when I heard his heavy footsteps and booming voice, I crept out of my room to look over the banisters. There was Uncle Sean, big and redfaced, rifle in hand, shouting at Aunt Maire — I scurried back.

My greatest delight there was to get into the dairy and bend over the large, deep earthenware brown pans. I would reach down and skim the cream with my fingers from the top of the milk — it tasted so good. My cousins threatened to report me to Auntie, but I went on doing it whenever I knew she was out of the way. Those were some of the most carefree days I ever spent.

I loved the seaside too, and the sand dunes where it was so easy to hide away and build dream-castles, but that roaring monster the sea frightened me with its big white-horse waves, and I refused even to paddle. Once a young, stupid nursemaid had picked me up in her arms and thrown me in — it was many years before I ventured in again and learned to swim. And once when the tide was a long way out, I went with a group of other children to meet it and we played for a time at the water's edge until someone noticed that the sea had crept right round us. The others, who were much taller, scrambled through the water to safety, but I was terrified and sure the rising water would overwhelm me. My screams were heard at last and one of the older ones came back and carried me on his shoulders to the shore, but I shall never forget the feeling that I was abandoned to drown.

We were a rather snobbish family, though there are some who would say we set our sights too high, considering that we did not always have the money to support our social inclinations. There were some children with whom I was not allowed to play, although in time it was to be the other way round and parents would forbid their children to play with me, for I grew wilder and wilder.

II

AFTER a few years of the convent school, when I was about thirteen, my mother decided that my term reports were quite hopeless. She thought it would be a fine thing to send me to a school she had heard about in England, which gave special care to what they called 'difficult' children. It was in one of the nicest places in England, an old market town with a famous cathedral, a slow-moving sedgy winding river beside which we loved to walk, and farming countryside round. I remember the dark fields of sugar-beet, and a grassy hill down whose slopes we rolled with great delight, and the October fair held in the market place, with its wonderful sideshows – oh, the excitement of setting off in crocodile, under the care of the nuns, with the pennies jingling ready in our pockets!

On the long summer evenings one of my delights was to go fishing, in the small stream that wound its way through the school grounds, for tiddlers. They would come along, a whole school of them, twenty or thirty at a time, quite unaware that above on the grassy bank stood a little girl ready to ensnare them. The long piece of string in my hand was attached to a big glass preserving jar. The baby fish who swam into it all unsuspecting would shortly find themselves on the classroom window-sill for our nature study. I may add that when inevitably they passed away, they got a most decent religious burial, with match-box coffin, flowers and tombstone.

Altogether, I was to spend two years there, although after the first, my mother, feeling that I was too far away from home, decided I should go back to Ireland. I was so unhappy and pined so to go back that she allowed me to return. It was not for long, however.

It happened like this. One Sunday afternoon, we were coming out of church when I saw the collecting plate in the porch with its glitter of silver. It was too much for me: with a quick look round to see that there were no adults in sight, I dipped in my fingers and brought up what to me seemed a huge sum, a six-pence. Some of the other girls had seen me and gathered round, shocked by my daring, so I said I would share it with them. On our way back, we went into the little local sweet shop and had a good old time buying long sticks of liquorice, sherbet, aniseed balls and so on. In those days, you could get quite a lot of goodies for sixpence.

When we were putting our coats away one of my friends rushed up to tell me I had been reported by one of the other girls. I did the first thing that came into my head, I took to my heels and ran out of school. Then I stopped to think. Where was I to go? Home was much too far away, but my half-sister was living in Dorchester: her husband was at Dorset. I had no idea where Dorchester was, but I thought if I took any train it would be sure to go there. I had no money, but I set off for the station.

At the barrier, the ticket-collector put out his hand to punch the ticket I did not possess. I said my mother was just behind with it. He gave me a long look, but he let me through. The first hurdle was passed, but what was I to do next? Perhaps I could hide under a carriage seat, and jump out quickly at the stop—I was not quite clear which, but I supposed it would be the first one the train came to. I paced up and down and no train came. The ticket collector seemed to be keeping rather a sharp eye on me. I walked to the far end of the platform, and as I turned back I saw at the barrier two of the lay-teachers from the school.

I had no idea how they had known where to find me, but there seemed nothing for it but to go over to them. With hardly a word, they took me firmly and marched me back to school.

Mother Superior met us, and told me to go straight to the Infirmary, where I would be punished. As I went along the corridors and up the stairs I saw several of my friends, but they did not speak to me. It seemed I was really in disgrace this time.

I sat down on one of the beds. After a period which seemed endless, Mother Superior came through the door looking very stern.

'Take off your clothes,' she said.

'All of them?' I stammered.

'All of them.'

I was trembling with fright and cold.

'Now lie face down on that bed,' she ordered. She picked up a cane which lay ready on a side table, ran her fingers along it and then gave me stroke after stroke, till my whole body was red and purple with weals.

I screamed and I roared, and the more I yelled, the more I was caned. Finally she told me to get into the bed – I was to stay there until my mother, who had been sent for, arrived in England to take me away.

In the end, it was two weeks before I left, and in all that time I was confined to the Infirmary. I was put on a train in the guard's care and my mother was to meet me at Waterloo. As I sat in the corner of a crowded carriage staring out of the window and trying not to catch the other passengers' eyes because I felt so ashamed, I wondered just what she was going to say to me.

Surprisingly, my mother must have sensed how upset I was. She was standing by the barrier, and she said nothing about my disgrace, but took me back to her hotel, where she made sure I had a jolly good tea. Then that evening she took me out to see a play – my first London play, but I can remember nothing about it but its name, 'It's a Boy', and the fact that Leslie Henson was in it.

I had not returned home for the holidays during my time in England. A few of the other girls stayed at school too during those times, which were really quite enjoyable. Sometimes parents would come and stay for a time in a guest house and take us out to seaside resorts like Weymouth or Bournemouth. In fact, I liked the school, liked my friends and even liked my lessons – whatever education I now possess, I owe to that place. For those who were in charge of me, however, my time there must have been anything but happy. I was always finding something to distract not only myself but the rest of the class, so I am quite sure that law and order must have descended over the school after my expulsion, and that goes for all the schools I attended.

I do not want to bore you with an account of them all, but I must mention my last one. It was a kind of domestic training school on the borders of South-East London, run mainly for mentally retarded girls considered in need of care and attention, though not in the legal sense. I must then have been fifteen, and I stayed there about eighteen months, with breaks in the summer by the sea at Herne Bay, where the school had a holiday house. This school, like all the others, was run by nuns, but this Order was most kind and understanding. They were specially trained to prepare difficult or abnormal girls for the battle of life, and for coping with the world. If only I had known at the time just what would come my way to cope with, I believe I would have stayed right there by the side of those good nuns, but at that time, I was raring to go as soon as I arrived, and longing only to be old enough to be allowed to leave schools forever.

We were taught domestic arts such as cookery, laundry work and dressmaking, but again, it was all wasted on me. I refused to concentrate, and the nuns seemed to allow me to come and go much as I pleased: in fact, I think they spoiled me, and I liked it — it was such a change from my other schools. During all the time there, I was never caned — it was the first time in my life that punishment had not hung over me.

At home, the cane had occupied a prominent place. In my early teens, much of my time was spent looking for its hiding place so that I could burn it or break it into small pieces. It was no good, however. Mother always bought a new one, and it seems as if there were always long red marks on my body. The other members of the family had also been in their day caned when they deserved it, but none of them was caned more often than me, and the more I was caned, the more rebellious, bold and disobedient I became. At the domestic science school, however, there was none of it — it was all very happy, but at last my wish was granted and I was allowed to leave.

School days were over!

.   .   .

After I had been idle for a month or so, my mother thought that I should now start to make some sort of career for myself. She suggested that I should take a course in nursery-nursing, a three-year course in Liverpool, once again run by nuns. The fees were high, but she was willing to make the effort, to see me settled in some kind of job. We were trained in a nursery school which was divided into a day- and a residential-nursery. It was in one of the poorest depressed areas, and usually both parents were out at work. They paid only sixpence a day at the day-nursery, and for this the children got very good value. When they arrived in the morning, they were given a bath, clean house-clothes, a glass of warm milk (or a bottle-feed if their age demanded it), a two-course dinner and all the care and attention of both trained and trainee nurses. The babies spent their day in cots in the nursery or, if the weather was fine, in prams out in the garden.

The older ones played games and rested on small stretcher-beds in their nurseries or out in the sun.

The parents collected their young at four-thirty p.m. — it always seemed rather absurd that we had to change the children back from clean clothes into their own dirty torn ones just before their mothers arrived! Life in the residential-nursery was run on much the same lines, but the children there were often boarded for quite long periods.

I only stayed there three months. I did not get on with the other nurses, perhaps because I was not yet ready to take on any kind of responsible job. But back in Ireland I was not unduly worried at still having no career, or at all unhappy; far from it. There were my boy friends.

.   .   .

There had for a long time been the schoolboys with whom I would pet and play during the long summers. We went as far as we possibly could without having actual intercourse, but it was chiefly curiosity: I had no real idea what it was about. We would lie stark naked in a summer-house or some secluded corner of the garden away from adult eyes, and play with each other's bodies. At times, there were two or three boys with me and I the only girl, and to my affection-starved soul this was wonderful. They would kiss and cuddle and touch me, exploring every part of my body. My family was unbelievably blind to the fact that these sessions were going on under their very noses.

Then there were the grown-ups, men friends of the family and old enough to be my father. Like the schoolboys, the older men would play around with me, but in a far more experienced way. Also, because of my tender age, they took care not to have actual intercourse with me. My reward for these long sessions was generally a large box of chocolates — the question of money never arose. For my part, I think I enjoyed this love-making also for the attention it brought me, short-lived though it might be. These older men for the most part had wives and children of their own. Mother did not dream what they were doing, and I was not going to enlighten her. I was enjoying myself, and the chocolates were so very good.

Joseph particularly was what one would call a real dirty old man. He was a professional man of some sort, and he was married — his wife was an invalid.

His great delight was his garden, not without cause, for in summer it was one mass of flowers. Often we would pick large bunches of these as a sort of camouflage for his indecent acts with me. He would take me into the summer-house or, if his wife was away, into the house, and strip me and play with me. Sometimes I cried out for him to stop, and then he had to, for fear the neighbours heard me.

Joseph also never went so far as actual intercourse, but he told me that when I grew up, when I was a big girl, he would, and I would like it. We moved shortly after to another district, and some years later when I really was grown up, I met him, quite by accident, in the street. I pretended not to see him, for he was on the opposite side of the road, but the next thing I knew, he was beside me raising his hat and greeting me. I did not want to have anything to do with him, but it was a main street, so I had to be polite and grown-up and make conversation with him. He reminded me of the sessions we used to have together and said that now I was a young woman he would like to keep his promise. I blushed and made no reply, so he asked if I would meet him at the cinema that evening. I would have promised anything to get rid of him. I did not turn up, and I never saw him again.

There was one older man, however, who was quite different from the rest. I thought him a little mad. Don was a bachelor. He was the owner of a large house standing in its own grounds. He was looked after by a housekeeper, and he had a large car.

When I was away at school, he would often send me pocket money, for he was very wealthy. When I was at home, I spent more time with him—my mother made careful enquiries into his character and felt she could trust him, as well she might. At weekends, we went out to country hotels and clubs for meals, riding and tennis lessons for me—for which he paid—and we would play tennis together. The evenings were spent at his house listening to music or dancing, or playing the Red Indian game.

This was how it was. We each held a dagger and went down on our hands and knees. Don would hide behind a large armchair and I, perhaps, behind the radiogram. Now came the preparations for the attack—we would try to stab one another all over the body. Whenever I was killed outright, Don would get hold of my leg and play with it from the toes up to the thigh but never any further. When it was Don's turn to be killed, he would lie flat on the floor and I would just let him lie there, for I did not relish the thought of playing with such an old man—and one not in any way handsome. Although he had plenty of opportunities to take other liberties with me, he never did.

Later, there was the coloured student at the university who took me to his room when his landlady was out. He got me on the bed and had intercourse with me to his entire satisfaction, although I still remained intact. I had to be terribly careful never to be seen with him, for if my family had found out, I think the fact that he was coloured might have seemed worse to them, with their typical way of looking at things, than my misbehaviour.

I never, as a young girl, had a special or lasting friendship with other girls, although I knew lots of them and went to their parties. On the whole, I was left very much on my own, for I really was very wild. Besides, I was different from them, for I knew the facts of life from experience long before they did. On rare occasions I played round with other girls. For the most part, however, I wanted to be with men.

III

I WENT through a phase of trying to attract the young university students. I would dress nicely, not too flashily, and arming myself with technical books, I wandered in and out of the university just as though I had the fullest right to be there. No one questioned me—they seemed to think I was one of them and that was just what I wanted to be. All the girls I used to know were now attending universities; I was the only one who had not made the grade. So I wandered along the corridors, in the grounds and into the coffee bars the students frequented.

Life at home meanwhile was one long round of rows, usually brought about by my refusal to find myself some sort of job. The only thing I had ever wanted to do was to go on the stage or dance, and that to my mother's way of thinking was worse than no job at all. Then again, I was kept very short of money. I rarely remember being given pocket money except when I was away at school. My clothes were nearly always my older sisters' cast-offs. Once when I was invited out for tennis, I found myself with only one pair of white socks, which were so small for me and so darned that I was ashamed to go out in them. I went into a large store where my mother had an account, bought a new pair—I remember they cost just two and six—and charged them to her. It was many months before I heard the last of that.

Sometimes when I desperately wanted money, I would go through my mother's and sisters' handbags, but they soon learnt to lock them away. Sometimes I would sell the tickets sent through the post by various charitable causes—needless to say, no money was returned to the society concerned. Then again, I would take books from their shelves and sell them to second-hand shops for a shilling or two. Sometimes I would take a valuable book without knowing it, and when it was missed, I would be questioned and questioned. I did not dare to admit what I had done, and there would be a family trek round the bookshops to try and find the book and buy it back again.

Then one day I found myself completely without money—not a penny. I suddenly decided to break into the house next door, which belonged to a solicitor and his wife. All day long I watched it, watched as the husband went off to his office, watched as the wife set off with her dogs and the maid-companion for their afternoon walk. This was the moment I had been waiting for.

Under a doormat, I found the key—it was all so easy. In I went, then up the stairs, having first gone through the downstairs rooms without much success. In the bedroom, I found a few shillings which I put into my pocket, and then I came across some jewellery, a diamond ring and a brooch, though at that time I did not realise what they were. I thought they might be of some value, however, and slipped them into my pocket too, then I left the house, picking up a large slab of chocolate from the hall table as I went.

There was no one at home when I got back. I sat down to think what to do with the jewellery. I remembered seeing a shop in town which had a notice saying they offered high prices for jewellery, so I decided to try my luck there.

Naturally, I was feeling very nervous, as I had never done anything of the kind before. I went into the shop and an old man asked if he could help me. I handed him the ring and brooch, and he asked me how much I wanted for them. I was quite unprepared for that and stammered something about 'whatever he thought best'. He looked from me to the jewellery and back to me again, and he handed me thirty shillings. I took it thankfully: I was too young to know that the real value was some hundreds of pounds.

Outside the shop I breathed a great sigh of relief. Supposing he had been suspicious of me and had called the police! But all was well, and I had thirty shillings in my pocket. I went straight off to the shops, and the first thing I bought was a hat—green velvet with a turned-up brim, very fashionable, very smart: it cost a whole pound. The rest of the money was very soon spent too, on tea, cakes and sweets, so now I was back where I started, and what was more, I had no doubt that sooner or later I would have to face the music.

Next morning, when I went out of the house to the little shop round the corner, I noticed two men who looked like policemen in plain clothes. They let me pass, but I felt them eye me closely.

That evening Mother told us of the robbery next door—the police had called at all the houses in the road, and they would be coming back that evening to interview every member of the family—they had told her they were questioning other households too.

We had just finished our evening meal and we were all rather tense at the thought of the coming ordeal, although no one had the slightest suspicion that I was the culprit. The door-bell rang, and I dropped the sugar-bowl I was just handing round: the sugar went everywhere. Into the middle of this confusion the two plainclothes men were shown in. They refused coffee and got straight down to business, though I felt their eyes turn to me every now and then. My mother and three of my sisters were living at home at this time. The two men questioned them carefully. All of a sudden one of them leaned across and, looking me full in the eye, said:

'Well, young lady, it certainly wasn't one of your sisters.' All eyes were turned on me. I felt the blush rising up my face, but I answered defiantly:

'Well, it wasn't me!'

Still everyone was looking at me. The detective asked if he could speak to me on my own in another room. No matter what he said, I still refused to admit anything. At last, my stubborn denials got him really annoyed.

'Look,' he said, 'I'll give you one more chance to tell the truth. Did you do it?'

'No,' I said again, and he started to walk back to the drawing room, saying that it would be much worse for me now, since I had not confessed the truth.

Suddenly I cried out. 'Come back! I did take the jewellery! I'm sorry!'

He left me in the hall outside with the other detective. I would have made a break for it if I could, but it seemed impossible. I tried to imagine what was going on behind the closed drawing room door. After a bit I could hear my mother crying, and my sisters trying to comfort her. Then the detective came out and without my being able to say goodbye to the others, he showed me to the front door: my mother and sisters did not come out to see me or reassure me.

Round the corner, a discreet distance from the house, the police car was parked. Sitting in front was the driver and in the back was an old man. I recognised him at once as the man from the jewellers'. One of the detectives got into the front seat; I was put in the back with the other. I looked at the old man and said, 'I know you.' He made no reply. Halfway to the police station they dropped him near a bus-stop: he was not needed any more. We drove on in silence.

When we arrived, I was really frightened, although the two detectives were most kind and polite to me—I think perhaps they were both family men, and I felt I had their sympathy. It was a large imposing building, the main city police station adjoining the Central Court. That was no consolation, however—to me a police station was much the same thing as a dungeon.

When I had been taken into the charge-room and formally charged, the station sergeant moved forward to take me to a cell for the night, but I broke out into loud screams, crying as if my heart would break. I rushed to one of the detectives and threw my arms around him: he tried to calm me and told the sergeant to go gently with me.

Never as long as I live will I forget the night spent in that police cell, the long, long hours alone, listening to the nearby court clock chiming the hours and half-hours. I lay back on a hard board covered by a hard mattress, with a hard pillow, and with an old blanket over me. I tried to sleep, but sleep would not come, for I was sobbing all the while. Where were my mother and sisters? Why had they let me come alone like this? I thought they were being cruel, but I was wrong, for they were working very hard for me behind the scenes, seeking advice from legal friends.

Through the small slit of a window in my cell I could see the dawn breaking and kept wondering just how long it would be before someone came to me. The hours seemed endless until there was the rattle of keys in the lock and a kindly woman, a police matron, came and took me into her own small room, where she made me some tea and toast. I could not eat, but I took the tea: I was longing for a cigarette.

It must have been about nine-thirty when the two detectives appeared. I was glad to see them. They told me that in twenty minutes or so we would be going into court. Oh dear. I asked if they could give me a cigarette. They looked at me in surprise— I suppose they thought I was a bit young to be smoking. However, one took his case from his pocket and offered me one, his last

—the other smoked a pipe. It was like manna from heaven, that cigarette: I drew in the smoke and felt steadier.

It was time to go into the court room. The proceedings are a complete haze to me now—I remember only that I was not put in the dock, but asked to sit down on a seat. My name was not called—probably because I was under age—but when the clerk of the court asked if the young lady was present, the detective silently pointed a finger in my direction. The magistrate leaned forward and he and the clerk had a long whispered conversation. Then, turning to the detective in the witness box, he nodded his head and said 'All right.' So the court proceedings were over. I have often wondered since why the solicitor from whose house I took the jewellery allowed the prosecution to go forward.

I had still another ordeal to face, however, for I was to be taken before the court doctor for a medical report. In the doctor's room there were five people, the two detectives, my mother, the doctor and me. I sat down, and the doctor said 'Good morning' and told me to dry my eyes. He then asked me to explain to him why I was now before him. He looked very stern and I did not take to him. Rebelliously I answered, 'There's no need to ask me—it's all written down on that paper in front of you.'

He did not like my reply. Turning to my mother, he said, 'I can find nothing at all wrong with your daughter.'

My mother burst into tears—that meant, of course, that there was nothing to prevent my being sent to a detention centre. When I saw her cry, I burst into tears too. In the midst of all this, the door opened and my elder sister came in.

She was now married and living the other side of the county. As soon as I was taken to the police station, my mother had phoned her. Her brother-in-law was an eminent State Counsel, and it was he who had arranged for a solicitor to represent me and asked for a medical examination. And now, this morning, my sister had driven over as soon as she could to be with us at court.

She and the doctor recognised each other at once, for they had often been partners at bridge, and they talked animatedly of the people they knew. After a few moments the doctor turned back to my mother.

'I have decided to send your daughter away for one month's rest to a hospital,' he said, and that was that. I had been lucky, or so I thought at the time.

And now I had to say goodbye to my mother and sister. The hospital was only two miles away, but my mother was loath to leave me, seeing how distressed I was. A kind good friend of the family gently guided her away to a waiting car to take her back home with her. The two detectives came with me as far as the hospital, and patting me in a fatherly way on the shoulder, wished me good luck — one of them even handed me a packet of cigarettes. Then I was on my own again.

IV

I STILL do not feel able to talk about my time in the mental hospital, which in the event turned out to be considerably longer than a month.

When it was over, my mother decided I must not come home, as the affair would need a long time to die out. It was arranged that I should spend a few weeks at a guest house by the sea, to decide what I wanted to do about my future. I thought I would like to go to France as an au-pair girl – I thought looking after children would be easy. So with the help of an agency, and armed with the family blessing, and a suitcase bulging with new clothes, I set out.

I sailed from Southampton to Le Havre, to join a family on holiday at the Normandy seaside resort of Cabourg. After the summer, I was to return with them to their home in Paris. There were three young children, a boy of six, a girl of five, and a new baby, who was not to be in my care at present. They had already had an English au-pair girl, who after three years with them was leaving to get married. They had thought very highly of her: she was proficient in every way regarding the care of children – they were in for an unpleasant shock over her successor! She had also spoken French fluently, whereas I did not know one word of it.

At Le Havre, I changed onto a small steamer to Deauville. I had been told to take a bus from there to Cabourg, where I would be met. As I stepped off the boat, however, I saw a long line of taxis. I was carrying a large, heavy suitcase and various bits and pieces, and I thought this would be a much easier way to travel, so I crossed over and tried to talk to a taxi-driver. As I had no French and the driver no English this was difficult. At last, however, he understood what I wanted, and wrote down the fare to Cabourg: it was a matter of some thousand francs!

I picked up my suitcase and found the way to the bus station. The bus was already packed, but a man offered me his seat. I thanked him in English. Everyone seemed to know everyone else and they were all talking and laughing together. I felt rather shy and out of things, and kept my face glued to the window-pane, watching the strange countryside go by.

The conductor came round for the fares, and once more I was in difficulties. Someone who spoke English came to my aid, and he also arranged with the conductor to see that I got down safely at my destination. It was a rough, bumpy, rattling journey; the bus was sweltering. Everyone round me wore summer frocks, open-necked shirts and shorts, but I was correctly dressed in a heavy tweed suit. There was nothing to do, however, but to sweat it out.

At Cabourg all was in confusion; people milled round the bus laughing, shouting, calling, and I was caught up in the middle of this crowd and for the life of me, I didn't know how I was to find Madame Jouvert, who was meeting me. I spent an anxious ten minutes, but then a tall, dark and attractive woman stepped up to me and introduced herself. She must have been in her early forties, quick and nervy, and typically French.

I could see that her first impressions of me were far from good. She had introduced herself to me by speaking English — very good English. She averted her eyes from my chaotic luggage and we began to walk the short distance to their villa. I was not at my best: it was so hot, and my town clothes and high-heeled shoes stuck to me. She walked very fast — luckily that made conversation difficult — but it took me all my time to keep up with her.

The villa was large and old-fashioned, with tall iron gates, long double windows, green shutters and wrought-iron balconies. There were five floors, each let to different married members of the family. Each group brought their children, their nurses, governesses, cooks, housemaids and so on. We arrived in time for lunch. They all dined together, so we were a large number. I was introduced to Madame's husband and children, and then to all the other members of the family. I felt strange, awkward and inadequate, the target for all their eyes. Not one of those sitting at table could speak English, with the exception of Madame. It was a pretty bad start.

All through lunch, the boy and girl I was to look after kept giving me defiant looks, as much as to say 'We don't like you, and we aren't going to like you'. They had both been very fond of the previous girl, but then she could get through to them, because she could speak French. I knew then and there that the family was not going to put up with me for long. I could not think how I would manage at all.

The children and I had our apartments on the second floor. Marie and I shared the same room and Jean was on his own. I had the normal duties—washing, ironing, taking them for walks. Most of the time was spent sitting on the bench while they bathed or joined in keep-fit classes with the children of all the other families who, like them, spent every summer by the sea at Cabourg. When Jean and Marie would not do what I told them, I smacked them hard—which in no way improved our relationship; they were not to blame, for they could scarcely do as I asked when they could not understand what it was I was saying. As a result, they were continually running to their parents complaining that I had beaten them or been cruel.

      .   .   .

On my days off, I got right away from the family. I went out with another English au-pair girl who lived nearby. She was older than me and considerably more mature. She had been a friend of the last au-pair girl at the villa. One day she reported that she had met two very handsome Italian medical students, and had made a date for us both with them at the casino on the promenade that evening. I was delighted. They really were handsome, as it turned out, particularly mine, whose name was Gino.

The courtyard of the casino was edged with little tables. We hardly sat at ours at all. We danced and danced under the coloured lights, with a black velvet sky beyond, and I grew more and more excited. Gino whispered in my ear that we should get away from the crowd of dancers, and I was beginning to feel that I wanted nothing more than to be alone with him. We watched our chance and gave the other pair the slip, and walked over the promenade and out onto the deserted beach. The day had been very hot, but now there was a slight breeze coming in from the sea, and my light linen frock felt just right.

We lay down on the sand and kissed and embraced and held each other tight as if we would never let go. Whatever it was that Gino wanted, I was ready to give, and give I did—it was wonderful! In spite of all the men who had played around with me, I had till now remained technically a virgin, but now I was one

41

no longer. I did not in any way feel I had lost anything: quite the contrary—I knew I wanted Gino to repeat the session again and again and again.

With all our passion spent we made our way back to the casino and began dancing once more. I noticed after a while that people kept looking me up and down, especially the men, in a knowing way. My girl friend seemed embarrassed when I spoke to her. She would not say what was wrong, but kept repeating that she thought it was time we went home. Even Gino's friend was giving him some very dirty looks. How was I to know that there was a large patch of blood on the back of my white frock, and that it was obvious to everyone that I had lost my virginity? It was not until next day that my friend told me what had happened and rushing to my wardrobe, I found she was speaking the truth.

Now it was the turn of Gino and his friend to be worried. They and the other girl always seemed to be in conference over me. At last, Gino told me that if I were pregnant, they would be able to do something about the matter, but I could hardly tell at that stage. I was not, as it turned out, but for weeks after, my friend kept giving me worried, anxious looks. It was kind of her, but she thoroughly embarrassed me and I felt it really was my own business.

That was the end of the affair, for I never saw Gino again. It was, I suppose, the beginning of the road.

.   .   .

I had been with Madame Jouvert and her family for about two months when I decided that, for the sake of both sides, the time had come for us to part. The last straw was one day on the beach when Marie, who had been running helter-skelter along the water's edge, tripped over a rusty old iron bar and broke her nose. Oh dear, the roars and screams of her. I was panic-stricken —whatever should I do? Luckily her father had just come down for his daily swim. He rushed up, lifted her in his arms and carried her back to the villa. Marie sobbed and yelled and every-one was standing and staring as though I had committed a murder. Madame heard her from afar and rushed to the window —I can see her now, white-faced and agitated and wringing her hands. The doctor was sent for. He reset the nose under ether.

I was in complete disgrace—no one would talk to me. They gathered in little groups, whispering in a language I still could not understand. I felt I could stay in the house no longer. I thought I would go to Paris and try to find another job, but this time with only one child to look after.

When I told Madame I was leaving, she did not seem sad about it, but both she and her husband were very worried at the idea of my going alone to Paris. It was not a place for one so young. They thought (and they were dead right) that I was incapable of looking after myself. In the end, they made arrangements for me to stay in an English students' hostel run by nuns. So I said a formal goodbye to the family, and an affectionate one to the English girl and set out for Paris.

.　　.　　.

The train journey was long and slow. I arrived just after midnight, a dangerous time for a girl on her own. I hailed a taxi driver and showed him the address of the hostel. He closed the door on me and my luggage, not before his greedy little eyes had looked me up and down devouringly. As we set off, he asked me in very broken English if I had ever been to Paris before. I said 'No' and then began to wonder whether he might kidnap me. I need not have worried, however. In a very short time we drew up at the hostel, and I saw the head of the nun who was waiting up for me peep from behind the window curtains.

I was to share a large bedroom with five other girls. The younger ones were quite friendly, but the older ones were hostile. Some had been governesses in very good French families and were now getting to the stage where they had to compete with younger applicants, so they vented their feelings on the younger girls in the dormitory. Although the charge for residence was quite high, the food was lousy, but I put up with the place because it suited me as a stepping stone to another job.

Paris itself I fell in love with from the start. It seemed such a clean fresh sort of city, and somehow it made me feel free. In between looking for jobs, I travelled all over it on foot or by bus—standing on the back because it was cheap and I saw better. One glorious summer day, I thought I would read in the park. I found a quiet seat in the Bois de Boulogne, but I did not open my book. I was fascinated by the endless motor traffic—it seemed that the whole world was going by. I had dressed in a tight white sweater and skirt, and must have looked quite attractive. After some time I realised that solitary drivers kept passing and repassing me, looking at me very hard. Then one after another they began to pull in at the kerb. At first they just sat in their cars in front of my seat, but much as I would have liked to be picked up, I had not quite got the nerve. Then they would get out and sit down by me. Those who could speak a little English explained that they wanted to make love to me and offered me money. They could not understand why I refused, and at that time I did not realise that a young girl alone on a park seat in Paris sits there for only one purpose.

The sister in charge of the hostel also ran an employment agency for au-pair girls and governesses. I was pleased when one wet afternoon she called me down from my room to tell me that she thought she might have a job for me. An employer was calling to interview several girls at the hostel. There were about six of us, the others people who would in every way have been far more capable and responsible for the job than I was, but such is life, I was chosen.

My new employer was Australian, a really smart, well-educated woman, married to an Italian musician. They had only arrived in Paris that morning from Florence, in a very great hurry — it was 1938 and looking back, I realise their speed must have had something to do with the political situation. I was to live with them in a hotel, having sole charge of their daughter Sarah, then just four years old. But I was once more back where I had started: whereas Madame and her husband could speak English, French and Italian, Sarah could only speak Italian.

I stayed with them some months, even moving with them to Switzerland at the time of the Munich crisis, but I was continually in hot water — there was always something I had not done, or something I had done wrong. In the end, it was the same as Cabourg: I gave notice just in time to prevent Madame giving me notice herself.

Back at the hostel, I had no need to rush into another job, as I had saved a little money by now. I took life easy, staying in bed a little longer in the mornings, walking in the parks, sitting in the cafés of the Boulevard St. Michel, talking and sipping coffee with the students from the Sorbonne, whom I got to know very well. They were handsome young men, much my own age, very gay and carefree, but in nine cases out of ten they were

44

also very poor. Their allowances only just covered their board and lodging and their university fees.

One day, when I had not one penny left and my current boy friend was also penniless, I sat on the edge of my bed in the hostel and racked my brains for a way to find some money. All of a sudden, I had an idea. I put on my outdoor clothes and set off for the Irish Embassy. Although it was only afternoon, the day's business was over. That did not deter me. Pushing open the big iron gates, I walked up to the huge front door and rang the bell. The door was opened by a commissionaire in a resplendent uniform, who informed me that the Embassy was now closed: I must call again tomorrow.

'I can't call tomorrow,' I said, 'I must see the Ambassador here and now. It is urgent.'

I must have impressed him; perhaps he thought I carried some diplomatic news. He opened the door a little wider. In I went, gliding over the most luxurious carpet, sinking down to a depth of about two inches. The next thing I knew, I was in a large study, standing before the Ambassador himself.

He also looked as if he could not quite make me out. He gave me a formal greeting and I introduced myself, producing my passport. I explained that I was in great need of money to pay for my board and lodging – which was untrue, as I had paid for them in advance – and that I was feeling very hungry. I made it all sound as sad as I possibly could. The Ambassador asked how much money I needed. I said I would very much like five hundred francs – it was not in those days a large sum of money, but I felt it was better not to overdo things.

Without batting an eye, he opened a drawer in his desk, started to count out some notes and then, with a smile, handed me the whole five hundred francs. I was really taken aback by his generosity and promised to pay him back – I am afraid he must still be waiting.

I did not let my mind dwell on the rights and wrongs of what I had done. My student friend and I went drinking and dining and dancing at an excellent restaurant, and it was a very gay, romantic evening. Then I was penniless once again. So what? Next day my boy friend was expecting to have some money from home and so we went on, share and share alike.

Shortly after this, I got myself a job giving English lessons to a young girl who lived with her family on what was then called the Boulevard Henri Martin. There was no paper work or grammar involved – I taught her as best I could by conversation. She was a charming girl – and like most French girls, heavily chaperoned by her mother. I managed to take her for tea and dancing to the American Students' and Artists' Club in the Boulevard Raspi, which she loved – I went regularly although I was not a member: with all my student friends, I just went in and out as I liked. Then I told her one day that I was going to a dance at the Cité de l'Université and she begged to come too, that is, if she could get her mother's permission. That was done, and we dressed ourselves up and went. There were some seven hundred couples there, all university students and their friends. It was very carefree and cheerful and some of the couples were dancing very close indeed, and those sitting out were cuddling and necking. It was great fun – we danced the conga in a long line around the hall, up the staircase and around the balcony. I was dancing the rumba and really letting myself go, and my charge was sitting out with a coloured student, when I saw her parents coming through the glass entrance doors. They took in the scene in one long sweeping glance and they did not like what they saw. They ordered their daughter home at once and that was the end of that job.

Life at the hostel went on much as usual while I looked for another. One day, I was waiting for a friend in the Metro and had arrived rather too early. I paced up and down, as I often do, and suddenly noticed an elderly woman of about forty, dressed in black, looking me up and down, smiling and bowing to me. I could not understand it – I had never seen her before in my life. She came over and spoke to me, and as I obviously could not understand her French, she began talking in English. She questioned me about where I was going, and who I was waiting for, then she asked:

'Wouldn't you like to come with me instead? I will find you plenty of men, plenty of wine, plenty of money!' She leered at me and I was very frightened. Luckily the train came in just then and she had to get on to it, but she kept looking back at me to see if I was going to follow her.

One grey, damp morning I was penniless again and was walking through the main shopping centre of Paris. I wandered into one of the large stores and looked and looked at the lovely clothes but there seemed little point – I could not afford any.

Suddenly on a rail I saw a heavenly evening dress, white organdie with a wide billowing skirt. It was a dream of a dress. An assistant came forward and asked if she could help me. I said I was just looking and she went away. It came into my mind that I could get it out of the shop under my coat. There was nowhere I could wear it, but that did not matter: I longed to have it so. I took it off the rail, but suddenly I could not go through with it.

The assistant was coming back. She went into a small office. I think perhaps she had seen me and was phoning for the manager. I hurriedly caught at the nearest object, tucked it inside my coat and made for the stairs. On my way down I saw someone who was obviously the manager or the store detective. I felt my legs trembling so that I thought I would never get past him. It was a long wide staircase, and as he came up he looked at me very hard indeed. I returned his stare calmly and walked safely past him with a stolen sweater under my coat. I would never have got away with the dress. I was very lucky indeed not to have found myself in a French prison.

The fright decided me. I packed up for home—not a moment too soon, for in a matter of weeks, war was declared.

V

I FOUND myself a room in a boarding-house in Swiss Cottage. It was only twenty-seven shillings a week, including my breakfast and dinner, but I was now running short of money and would have to find a job. Everyone was being patriotic and joining up, and I did not want to be left out. I loved England as much as anyone, for all I came from Dublin! I had at that time no great affection for Ireland—I had no kind memories of the people there. All the good things that have happened to me, all my real friends, have been in England.

I went to an Army recruiting centre, where I filled in some forms and found myself a member of the Women's Army Service —the A.T.S.—with orders to report in two days' time to an Army centre, where I would be allocated a billet and an office to work in. I was to do clerical duties, filing—I knew nothing at all about it, but I had implicit faith that the Army would teach me.

I never gave them time to train me, however—I was in and out in a matter of two weeks. I teamed up with a mother and her two daughters who had joined at the same time as me, a very restless and unstable pack. We shared the same billet—left to myself, I would have thought it a very good one, clean and with plenty of food. They were always complaining of it, however, though I suspect it was far better than anything they had been accustomed to. When they announced that they were coming out of the Army, I said I would leave too. It was a pity—I might really have learnt how to file and have been qualified for a job at last.

I returned to Swiss Cottage, to the boarding-house. It was very depressing: all boarded up with wood and sandbags and the windows hung with blackout curtains. There were some other tenants now, a German refugee family who had just escaped to England, a father and two daughters. I saw very little of them, for they did their own cooking on a gas ring in their room.

One evening, however, they persuaded the landlord to lend them his dining room and they gave a dinner party. I was upstairs all alone and feeling fed-up and bored with nothing to do. I wished I had some money. It occurred to me that the refugees' room was empty—I might find something there. I came out of my own room and stood on the landing for a moment, listening and looking to see if the coast was clear. I tried their door—it was unlocked. I switched on the light, after making sure the blackout was covering the window. I could see no money, nothing of any value. I opened the wardrobe and put my hand in: there was a suitcase there. I drew it out, and inside was a small knitting-bag. It seemed to be sewn up, but I was able to tear it far enough apart to get my fingers in. It was packed chock-a-block with jewellery, all gold, mostly watches. Quickly I took two of the watches and put them in my pocket, closed the suitcase, put it back in the wardrobe and fled back to my own room.

My first thought was to get away from the house as quickly as possible, but it was not far from midnight—it would be better to leave it until the morning. The dinner party was now breaking up and I could hear the guests departing. The family came upstairs to bed and went into their room. I kept my fingers crossed that they would not discover their loss.

In the morning, when I had dressed, I packed my bag, and with the two watches safe in my pocket, crept carefully past their room and down the stairs. The landlord was coming up and he was very surprised to see me, even more so when I told him I was leaving there and then. However, as I had paid him the week's rent in advance, there was nothing he could do.

I took a bus, suitcase and all, and checked in at a West End hotel, telling the receptionist I would pay her in the morning. I was foolish enough to telephone my ex-Army mother and daughters and tell them I had two watches I wanted to sell as I was short of money. Like a flash, they were round—they knew a good pawnshop and they would show me just where it was: we would go together.

The pawnshop was in Soho, and the man must have known these were no ordinary watches: he looked them over carefully with his watch-glass, and opened them up to examine their works. He only offered me two pounds for them, however—he probably realised I did not dare argue with him.

My ex-Army friends were waiting for me. They relieved me

of one pound note at once, saying how hungry they were. We went to their room, armed with a bag of fresh bread rolls, butter and bananas, and sat on a large double bed to have a good feed. That left me with just one pound note to pay my hotel bill. If they could have got that out of me too, they would have done, but I was firm and left them.

Next day when I had paid the bill, there was very little change. I had a cheap lunch in a cheap café, and bought a packet of cigarettes. Then I went into the lounge of another big hotel, and sat down to think what to do next. Later, in the ladies' cloakroom there, I first came across a girl called Bobby, a bottle-blonde, and much older and wiser in the ways of the world than I was. She told me she was living in a furnished room at the back of Marble Arch with an Indian medical student. She invited me back to her room, and that was the start of a sort of friendship. Singh turned out to be of good breeding and well-educated, quite different from Bobby, who was what I would call common.

Friendly as she was, however, Bobby did not offer to put me up for the night, although she knew that from then on I had nowhere to live and often had to sleep in railway-station waiting rooms. When I left them, I walked along the Edgware Road, and let myself be picked up by a passing motorist. I allowed him to play around with me – that was all he wanted – and he told me that if I liked, I could sleep in his car for the night: he would park it just round the corner from his flat in the Bayswater Road. I was very grateful, though I wondered what I should do if an observant policeman spotted me curled up on the back seat. It was pretty cramped, but there was a roof over my head, and I managed to get to sleep. I woke with the dawn, sat up and looked out. On the corner only a little distance away were two police officers. Down I went again on the seat, and curled up tight until they had gone.

After that, I spent many of my days in Bobby's flat – she was glad of the company when Singh was out. I haunted the nearby hotels too and often found someone to give me an evening meal or take me dancing. Sometimes I would spin them the tale and they would give me money for lodgings or food.

One evening I was coming out of Bobby's front door wondering where I was going to sleep that night when a young Indian in the same house, a waiter in a nearby restaurant, asked me up to his room for a drink. I did not like the look of him much, but I thought it might be somewhere to spend the night. We had our drink. The Indian looked rather dirty. We got into his bed and I noticed the sheets were absolutely black. That was a night! I never closed an eye. He mauled and pawed me, but every time he put his hand near my body, I felt revolted and kept moving and turning this way and that. He grew angrier and angrier as he realised I was not going to give him what he wanted. I was glad to see the dawn break at last, so that I could get away from him. I never told Bobby that I had slept with him.

One day, when we were sitting in her room having morning tea with rolls and butter and reading the *Daily Mirror*, I felt suddenly I ought to be doing more for King and country—I was not sure quite what, but the war news was bad: all the man-power and woman-power available was needed. I talked the matter over with Bobby and managed to make her see it was our duty to answer the call. Then and there, we decided to join the Land Army.

We made our way to the Land Army Headquarters, which were in Tothill Street, and were shown into the Recruiting Officer's room. She said at once that we were not the type of girl they required—we were far too soft for the hardships of country life. We assured her we were really very strong: if only she would sign us on, she would never have cause to regret it. So, somewhat against her will, she enlisted us in the Land Army and the very next day, we called to collect our uniforms.

It was a hideous outfit—I often wonder how I ever wore it, but at the time I felt very proud and confident in it. The war was about to be settled and won—by Maureen and Bobby—down in the Vale of Evesham.

Poor old Singh, he was very upset when Bobby told him that we were about to leave London and do our bit for the war effort. He tried in every way to entice her not to, but she had got her uniform and we were going. First, however, we had to find money for our fares, for though the Land Army would refund them at the other end, we had to buy our own train tickets there. Singh came up with Bobby's fare, but he couldn't find mine as well. Off I went to one of my hotels once more. A very nice man offered me dinner and when I told him about the Land Army he straight away gave me the money: we were all set.

With gas masks over our shoulders and identity cards in our pockets we set off for Paddington. At the station, we noticed other girls in the same uniform getting into our train, and we thought they must also be going to Evesham. The train was packed with troops, so we had a gay old time, laughter and chatter the whole journey. At Evesham we were met by some sort of Land Army captain and our employer and his wife. Our work was to be market-gardening – what that entailed, we were about to find out.

We were billeted in a council house, which to our distress had no bathroom – we felt it was a bad start. The food in the billet was really bad. We were supposed to receive a hot dinner at the end of our day, but it was always cold, and dished up – thrown up would be a better description – in a most unappetising way. The landlady was an old, rough, narrow-minded person, very uncouth, and from the first, she and I never saw eye to eye. I can say little about her husband, except that he was old too, for she kept him very much out of our sight – we wondered just which she did not trust, her husband or us.

Market-gardening was literally back-breaking work – our backs were bent double with hoeing, weeding and raking. When I was put on the job of slashing strawberries (though what strawberries had to do with the war effort, I never found out) I had my own method of saving my back. I would sit on the ground and as I went from strawberry patch to strawberry patch, without rising up I propelled myself along on my bottom. All the time that I was slashing strawberries, they never got a chance to grow, for as soon as I saw a red tint appearing I would pick and eat them, so that I am sure the crop must have been pretty poor that year.

Some evenings, when we felt we could not face the landlady's supper, we would go and have a good feed of chips. One evening we met two soldiers in the chip shop, and they asked us to go for a walk with them. My new friend and I – was his name Jim or Keith? I cannot now remember – were having a very good time and we were both getting very hot with passion and desire. Something would have to be done about it – at least Jim (or Keith) thought so, but although I was feeling hot, the desire was not all that pressing in me. Looking at my watch, however, I realised it was too late to go back to the billet, for the landlady would by now have bolted and barred the door. Jim (or Keith) said he knew where there was an empty Army tent we could sleep in. It was not a very pleasant night. I had not only to put up with the overtures of my soldier, but the creeping, crawling insects, for we were lying on the bare earth, no blankets or anything under us. I felt a nervous wreck by dawn — what Keith (or Jim) felt like I neither knew nor cared: now I had to face the return to the billet.

I walked along the street as slowly and softly as my Land Army boots would permit. Softly I went through the gate. The front door was slightly ajar: she must be up already getting her husband's breakfast — he went off to work very early. Slowly and softly I started to climb the stairs, but it was not my lucky day. Out she came from the kitchen and let loose on me with words. I just stood there and let her have her full say. There were no names she did not call me. When she had spent herself, I just went on up the stairs to the bedroom, without a word.

Bobby was about to get up. She seemed very fresh — after all, she had had a good night's sleep in a proper bed. That was exactly what I wanted, but instead, I had to wash and tidy myself up and go back to slashing strawberries. Was I glad to see my bed that evening!

It was the most wonderful summer weather during our weeks in Evesham, but we were getting very bored with the old landlady, no baths, no hot water to wash in. We gave notice, packed our bags and took the train to London. I must admit we felt embarrassed when we handed back our uniforms in Tothill Street, and their looks said plainly 'I told you so!' So we faded out of the Land Army and old England was still fighting the war in spite of our efforts to end it. Bobby returned to Singh, who was delighted to see her back, and for a time, they allowed me to sleep on a chair in their room. I had nowhere permanent to live, however, so at last I decided to return to Dublin.

The night before I had planned to leave I met a pilot officer in the Air Force — let us call him Lionel — in my hotel. He was tall, dark and very good-looking, about four years older than me, and I fell head over heels in love with him. I stayed on in London two or three days to be with him until the end of his leave, and when we parted, he took my home address and promised to write: he seemed quite as much in love with me as I was with him.

Back in Dublin, life was much the same as before I went to

France, little money, constant rows—only now I felt it much worse, as I had tasted independence. I spent a lot of time lying on my bed dreaming, for there seemed nothing else to do. I had no one I could talk to. It never occurred to me to go to our parish priest. I had got right away from religion, and he represented to me all the things my mother and family stood for, all the things I most disliked at that time.

I remember one Sunday feeling lazy and deciding, greatly daring, that no one and nothing was going to get me out of my bed that day to go to Mass. I lay there, despite frequent calls from my distracted religious mother, and listened to the front door and car doors slam as, one after the other, the family went off to the different morning Masses. Admittedly, as I lay with one eye and one ear open I felt horribly guilty, but I had determined to rebel against the family's so-called religion. I shall never forget that Sunday—as I had missed Mass, not one of the family would speak to me all that day! Our lunch was grim and silent, and I felt I hated them all more than ever.

In Dublin at that time there was one church which had a very late Mass, about 12.40 a.m. I think it must have been held for the benefit of hotel and club workers and other late night birds. It of course attracted anyone who had spent a riotous Saturday night—a lot of them looked as though they were suffering severe hangovers and would have been better off in bed! When I discovered this late Mass, I used to go to it. For me it had the flavour of rebellion and this I loved, because my mother strongly disapproved of it.

The weeks went by, and I had heard nothing from Lionel, my Air Force officer. I began to think our affair had meant nothing to him. I was very miserable and tried to put the thought of him out of my mind.

One Friday evening, when I came in from a game of tennis, I heard voices in the drawing room so I went straight up to my room, threw my racquet onto the floor and myself on top of the bed, because I was tired. After our game there had been dancing at the tennis club, and it had been fun. I heard steps outside my room, and one of my married sisters came in on tiptoe.

She told me in a whisper she wanted me to know what was happening as she felt I was being unfairly treated: letters had been coming to the house for me, which my mother had read and thrown on the fire. They were, of course, from Lionel, and apparently Mother was so upset and so determined I should not go to him as he had been asking, that the family was planning to have me certified and placed in an institution.

My sister said if she were in my shoes she would pack a suitcase, go back to London and marry Lionel, since that was what he was wanting. She even offered to give me a lift into Dublin if I would meet her along the road in about a quarter of an hour's time.

At this moment, my mother came upstairs and looked into my room. She gave my sister a hard glance, but said nothing beyond how disgracefully late I was coming home after tennis. They went down together and I quickly changed and slipped out of the house. I had no intention of accepting my sister's lift: I wanted to think first. I walked and walked for an hour or more along the darkened seafront. Well after midnight, I found myself passing the house of some friends from the tennis club. There was a little light in one bedroom, so after a moment's hesitation, I rang the bell — I was feeling very cold by then. There was a long wait, then my friends' father came to the door and was very surprised to find me there. I made up some story about being locked out of the house and unable to make anyone hear, and he insisted I should come in and sleep in their spare room.

The others were astonished to find me at breakfast next morning. I managed to say very little and set off to my married sister's. She gave me lunch and asked what I intended to do. I said I would slip home and pack a case, because I would be in straits if I went off, as I had by now decided to do, without even a toothbrush. Unknown to me, having made sure of my plans, she then phoned home and told them. My mother had been very angry when she found my bed not slept in, as she had guessed I had been warned, and she made my sister promise to help in the family plan after all.

I refused a lift back in the car and waited for a bus. It was a creeping, crawling bus, ahead of schedule, so it stopped at every second lamp-post. I was in a fine state of agitation when at last I got home. I tried the side door but it was locked. There was nothing for it but to try the front door boldly — but that was locked too and I had to ring the bell. One of my sisters came and pretended to be surprised to see me. The reception I received from the rest of the family was cold, in fact icy. I went up and began packing and my mother followed me. She warned me that if I intended to travel to 'that man', as she called him, she would have the police stop me as I was under age.

By now, I had all I needed and, suitcase in hand, I walked right across to where my mother stood and told her that if she did not move out of my way and let me go, I would murder her! She moved back quickly—she obviously believed me capable of it, and at that moment there was such hatred in my heart I think I might have done it. I walked downstairs and out of the front door, watched in silence by my mother and sisters, and there in the road was a friend of mine reversing her car. She waved and asked if I would like a lift into town and thankfully I jumped in. We passed two large and ominous black cars which turned into our drive—I was just in time. Now I really was on the run!

The friend could see my distress and asked if she could do anything, but I said no, I just wanted to go to my married sister's—I still did not believe she had changed sides. She was naturally very surprised to see me as she had expected I would have been detained, but she had enough sympathy not to let them know where I was. I got in touch by phone with my elderly friend Don, who agreed to lend me five pounds for my fare and expenses: his chauffeur brought it over very quickly and I set out for the overnight boat to Liverpool.

When I had known this boat in the past, it had always set sail quite late on Saturday night, to allow English theatre companies to return after their last performance of the week, but now, with the war, there were no foreign touring companies in Dublin, and the time of the boat's departure had been brought forward. As my taxi came in sight of the harbour, the driver pointed to the lights of the vanishing boat. 'Look!' he said, 'you've missed it!' I was very upset at the time, but it was a blessing in disguise, for I found out afterwards that the Eire police were keeping a sharp watch on the port to prevent my sailing.

My next move was to get the train over the border to Belfast: I did not want to stay a minute longer than I needed in Dublin. I went back to my sister and begged a bed for the night. She remarked somewhat sourly that I seemed to be missing everything that day, but she said I might stay. I was so frightened I might be caught, I asked if I could sleep under her bed in case they came looking for me, but she laughed at my fears and put me in the spare room, where after all I spent a good night.

I got up early and went for a taxi. It was Sunday, and there were none there. It was far too early for buses, so I rang a private car-hire firm, and in a matter of minutes, a beautiful black Daimler glided to a halt outside my phone box. I asked to be taken to the station, and just to be sure, I snuggled down well into the corner seat.

At the station approach, I had a dreadful fright. Two policemen had been lurking out of sight behind a large advertisement, and as we drove in, one stepped right out onto the kerb edge to take a look at the car. They let us pass. It was lucky for me there had been no ordinary taxis about because that was what they were expecting to find me in. The driver dropped me mercifully close to the ticket office, and I managed to get a second-class ticket to Belfast without seeing any more of the police.

That ticket was another stroke of luck: in those days, there were three classes on the Great Northern Railway. As I walked through the unguarded barrier, I saw the policemen talking with the guard by the third-class carriages far down at the end of the train. They saw me—they could hardly fail to do so, for few people were travelling at such an early hour, but they were obviously not expecting me to travel second-class. As casually as possible I found myself a carriage and settled down deep in a corner. After a while, I heard the policemen's voices coming along the platform and started to make a dive for the lavatory: I decided that if I was caught, I would jump out of a window and make a run for it, if I survived the fall! The policemen went past without so much as a glance at my carriage, however, and I began to feel a little better.

I got across the border without any incident, but when I reached Belfast, there was another hitch. There were no Sunday sailings, so I had to book into a small hotel for the night. I managed to borrow a pound to pay for it from a nice man I met there, who gave me dinner. At last it was time to board the ship. I took my place in the passport queue, but when it came to my turn, the officer told me I had no exit-permit stamp. I was very shaken. I asked if there was any way at all I could get one in time to catch the boat, and he said that if I went across to the harbour police station, just possibly they would give me one, even though it was so late at night.

I had to take the risk. I asked to see the Inspector and was shown into his office. He looked through my passport, then looked very hard at me.

'Are you by any chance running away from home?' he asked.

I gave him my best smile and said of course not—I was going to England to get a war job; so, after another long glance, he stamped my passport and I was free. Perhaps if I could have looked into the future, I would not have been so optimistic about the value of freedom!

In London, I made straight for the hotel where I had stayed with Lionel. (In those days, even at the best hotels, bed and breakfast cost only about eleven shillings a night.) I had no idea what to do next: nearly all my money was gone, and it was all very well coming over to find a husband—I had no idea of his address! I determined to write and ask the sister who had sheltered me for it. She replied with it by return. I suppose that now I had reached England, the family felt that the sooner I was made an honest woman, the better. It was many years before I had any more contact with my family after that: the break had been made.

VI

I WROTE to Lionel and had a telegram by return saying that he had managed to get leave and would be coming that evening to take me down to stay near his base. That was the first of many weekends there, when he had leave from flying, and whenever he could he came up to London for the day to see me. We did not get married then, however. He was afraid of what his parents would say, and in particular his mother, whose darling he was. She had set her heart on his marrying well.

I was not the first woman in his life. At home, he had fallen in love with a girl, but his family considered her beneath him, and the romance had to be kept very quiet. They used to go off to country hotels together, unknown to his parents, although Lionel was little more than a schoolboy and she was considerably older.

One day I thought I was pregnant — I was sure of it, though in fact it turned out to be a false alarm. Lionel said we would get married immediately and tell our parents afterwards, to avoid opposition. The first thing his mother and father knew of it was the telegram he sent them — and the first my family knew was when a friend who had seen the announcement I put in the Irish papers rang up my mother to congratulate her on the wedding of her youngest daughter. It must have been quite a surprise — but then, where I was concerned, she was always sure of surprises.

Until matters could be arranged, I was to stay with Bobby. Lionel rang me up there one morning and told me he had managed to fix up the wedding for the very next day. He was not able to get off duty, so he asked if I would buy the ring, and he would give me the money later. I got one from a shop in the Edgware Road for the large sum of fifteen shillings. I remember that in church, the vicar kept turning it over and over in his hands, as though he was trying to make out its gold content! Afterwards, as I was washing my hands in the cloakroom of the hotel where we had lunch, it slipped from my finger. The manager called in a plumber to get it out of the drain: I wondered if he would have gone to so much trouble if he had realised its true value!

We were to be married in the village church near Lionel's base, according to the rites of the Church of England – if he had suggested we should be married in a Buddhist Temple, I would have raised no objection in those days for my faith meant nothing to me. I asked Bobby if she would go with me as bridesmaid. I had no trousseau – just a new pair of silk stockings: I had neither spare money nor clothing coupons for more.

On the day itself, we were to take the nine-thirty train from Waterloo. As we reached the barrier, the gates closed on us and the train started to move out. It was all Bobby's fault. She had been so taken up with her boy friend, she had stayed in bed too long. I was terribly upset. I sent Lionel a telegram at his base, saying we would be late. As he had already left for the hotel where we were to meet, however, he did not get it until after we were married!

We caught the next train without difficulty, but when we arrived, there was only one taxi in sight, and that had been ordered by another passenger. We begged the driver to take us too, for he was going to the very hotel we wanted, but he refused. All he would agree to do was to come back for us when he had delivered his customer. I was in a terrible state once more, but at this point, his passenger came up, and when she heard our story, she offered to let us ride with her. She was the wife of an Air Force sergeant, and was so kind that she refused to let me pay our share of the taxi.

As we drew up at the hotel, I could see a distracted Lionel peering out of one of the windows – no wonder, for I was over an hour late, and the clergyman had been waiting at the church for us too. As I was thanking the sergeant's wife, Lionel rushed out with great relief and embraced me. He had been worried that I would not turn up, and that he would have had to stand the ragging of his fellow-officers.

The three of us set off for the church. Lionel went a little ahead, to make it look proper, for the bridegroom is supposed to be at the church first. When Bobby and I arrived, the verger was on the step looking very stern and angry at the delay. As for Bobby, for all her interest in what was happening, we could have been out for the daily shopping. There was no man to give me away, so I walked up the aisle—rushed would be more the word—with the verger and just stood at the altar rails by Lionel. The vicar had never seen me before in his life, and would never see me again. He asked me to produce my birth certificate. I had not got it with me, and it would have meant writing for it to Dublin. In the end, as Lionel was of age and an officer, the vicar took his word that I was of age too—just as well, as actually I was still only twenty, and would not have been allowed to marry without my mother's consent!

The service progressed, and the vicar gave us both a little sermon. At the time, I thought how nice it was: true, when he paused to find the right word, as he did rather frequently, I opened my mouth and supplied it for him, which rather horrified Lionel. When it was all over, the three of us walked back to the hotel for lunch. It was a very ordinary lunch, with cider to drink, no champagne, for it was the end of the month and Lionel's bank balance was rather low. Afterwards, the manager, who remembered me from my weekend visits, came over and said we should have told him we were getting married, as he would have given us a private room and a special meal. But there had been no time to let him know—like most things in my life, it was all such a rush.

Bobby left after lunch for the London train and her boy friend—she seemed bored with the whole affair. Perhaps she was also a little jealous of my good-looking husband in his smart uniform: I was so proud of him and so obviously in love.

Lionel and I then went for a walk in the countryside, hand in hand, and we found a little farm house where they did teas, and lingered over the meal a good hour. Then it was time for me to go back to London, for Lionel had explained he was to stand by at his base awaiting transfer. The train drew in, a blacked-out, dirty old war-time train, and we had to part. It was a very slow train, stopping even between stations. I could hear the drone of planes flying overhead, and I remember thinking they must be German. When at last we got to Waterloo, I jumped into a taxi to go back to Bobby's flat. As we went along I heard a strange noise, and my first thought was that it was a police car siren, and we were being gonged. I slid open the partition and asked the driver what was wrong. He said it was an air-raid—this was only the second occasion on which the sirens had sounded in London. He said he was making for the nearest air-raid shelter,

Hyde Park Corner. We drew up to the kerb, he jumped out, grabbing his gas mask, and called to me to follow him.

I sat still some seconds and he was lost to view. He had not even asked for his fare. I got out and said to myself 'To hell with him! I'm going to get back to the flat!' There was a police officer standing near, so I asked him what I should do—my taxi-driver had disappeared down the shelter and I had not paid my fare. He suggested I should forget that taxi-driver and call another taxi, so I did just that.

Between Hyde Park Corner and Marble Arch, the taxi was twice stopped by air raid wardens and we were told to pull in to the kerb. They were quite in order, for we had been told that if the sirens went, all traffic should come to a halt. However, I spun them some story about having to get home to my children and we were allowed through.

I found Bobby and her boy friend were about to retire for the night, but they said I might stay there a day or two. I didn't feel much like going to sleep, so I dressed in slacks and a sweater and went out to see what was going on. I walked down the street—strictly against the law during an air-raid—and was just about to turn round again towards the back of the Cumberland Hotel when I was grabbed by two air-raid wardens and taken down into a shelter, in spite of my protests. There were a few elderly men there and some women in minks and sables—I felt rather out of place! After half an hour, when nothing had happened, one of the wardens gave me a large wink, and I managed to slip out unnoticed and get back to Bobby's flat. So that was my wedding day and my wedding night!

Just after that, Bobby and her boy friend found a larger flat, in Paddington, where they promised me a room of my own. The flat was beautifully decorated and furnished; even the linen was provided. I began to feel happy in spite of everything. After only three days, however, Bobby announced without any warning that I must leave. Lionel had just moved, and had not had time to send me a letter giving his new address. I was in a quandary.

Opposite Bobby's flat was a small mews garage used as a private car-hire business: I got talking to the manager, and when he heard my difficulty, he let me spend the night there sleeping in one of his taxis. I wanted to catch the postman on his early round so that I could collect Lionel's letter when it arrived. Very early in the morning, this manager took me to an all-night café nearby and gave me a cup of tea and a roll: I was really grateful, as I was starving by then, but I remember the wonderful smell of eggs and bacon cooking, and how I longed for enough money to be able to buy myself some—Lionel had not thought to make me any allowance. When we got back, I was so busy talking to the manager that I nearly lost my letter. I looked up just as the postman was about to drop it through Bobby's letterbox. We shrieked at him, and he let me have my post. There was the letter from Lionel giving his address—now to get the fare to go after him.

I racked my brains how to get some money. I went down to Fleet Street, to the London offices of a big Irish newspaper, and managed to persuade them to let me telephone Dublin, on condition that when my money came I would pay for the call. I rang one of my sisters and with some difficulty persuaded her to telegraph me five pounds. It was at least an hour before we heard steps on the stairway to the office and the telegraph boy came in with my money order. I said I would cash it at the nearby Post Office, and the newspaper man asked if I would just leave my luggage while I did so—he must have realised I had been working out how to get away without paying for the call! However, I was very grateful to him for getting me out of my difficulty, so I paid up with a good grace, and then got a train to Lionel in the Midlands.

I had sent him a wire saying I was coming and asking if he would meet the train. He did—but I was not on it. I had forgotten to change at the right station. I got out finally at Doncaster and the station master explained how I could get back to my real destination by bus. He also telephoned the station where Lionel was waiting and caught him just as he was leaving, wondering where on earth I had got to.

On the bus, I asked for the right town, and the conductor wanted to know which stop. I had not the slightest idea, nor was I sure if Lionel would meet me—I said I would pay at the end of the ride. It was blackout time, and when I was able to peep out at the countryside, there was nothing to see but darkness. It was a very long journey and I wished heartily that it would end. There were only three other passengers—it was all very strange. A long time later we came to a halt at a bus stop and the conductor pushed back the door. A voice from the pavement outside asked if there was a young lady on the bus from Doncaster – it was Lionel.

We went to a hotel where he had booked me a room – he himself was officially living-in at the camp. That might really be called my honeymoon night. About a week later, Lionel enquired when I would be returning to London. It was the last thing I wanted to do. To my surprise I had found I really was pregnant now. Lionel himself had recently been billeted out in a farmhouse near his base but he had not asked me to move in with him. He went off on a short course to another part of the country and I took matters into my own hands and moved into the billet – there was already another officer and his wife, also pregnant, but older than me and with little else in common, in the house. Needless to say, Lionel got a surprise when he returned from his course to find me settled in, but he accepted the fact.

The farmer and his wife were very kind, though the farmhouse was not quite what I had been used to: for one thing, there was no indoor lavatory or bathroom. Lionel could get baths at the base, but if I wanted one I had to use a green canvas service contraption, in front of the fire.

At first I looked forward to the weekend leaves we spent down in Devon with Lionel's parents. They had a beautiful house with large gardens and tennis courts, and a beautiful view over the bay. We were given a quite separate part of the house which before the war had been the servants' quarters. Lionel's father was retired and very wealthy. His mother was Irish and a lapsed Roman Catholic, but she did not like to be reminded of either fact. She was a hard woman, much harder than my own mother, very capable and competent, and I was a terrible disappointment to her. She had been my father-in-law's housekeeper before he married her. After that he took in hand her education and they travelled all over Europe to see famous buildings and places. She was the greatest snob I ever met, and from the first seemed jealous of my being young and attractive. She was always picking on me at table and my father-in-law, who was very attached to me, would take my part. However, he died quite soon and things were never right for us again. My mother-in-law must take a large share of the blame, but I was really too young to be married then, and too immature.

As an example, I used to embarrass Lionel terribly when I lived near the base. Not at parties – I never attended above half a dozen official functions, but in not understanding that wives must not interfere in service matters. One dark night, Lionel went out on some sort of flying mission to inspect enemy lines. I had heard the planes and seen their lights as they flew over the hotel—I counted them: six in all. Two hours later they returned and I counted them again—only five! Lionel had arranged to come straight back to me when he landed. I waited anxiously, but he did not appear. I phoned the base and they said he had made a forced landing: they could give me no other news at present, but would contact me as soon as they knew more. I was terribly worried, however, and kept ringing and ringing, until the officers the other end were really fed up with me. I was always doing this sort of thing.

My pregnancy turned out to be a crisis in our marriage. I felt quite unready to cope with being a mother, and in a panic I told Lionel so. After a few days, he came and asked if I would like an abortion, because he had found someone who could arrange it. By that time, however, I had come right round to having a baby of my own to look after and love, and I was horrified by his idea, and hurt and shocked that he should have suggested it.

The nine months waiting period was a very long, lonely time. I had broken with my mother and family whom I might have gone to. War-time food was not the most suitable, and I was sick two or three times a day. There was another reason for that: at the farmhouse, they had got permission to kill a pig, and for weeks on end, sometimes three times a day, we ate some part of that pig. Whenever Lionel took me out in his car, I had to ask him to stop so that I could get out and be sick.

I was very turned in on myself and kept away from the other service wives who, not surprisingly, did not bother much with me as a result. I was terribly lonely, and when Lionel had to be away flying or on short courses, I would cry for him until I thought my heart would break. I spent my time collecting a large bottom drawer for the baby. I so much wanted it to be a girl and it was, the dearest mite in the world. It was due in February, and about a week before, Lionel announced that he had arranged to spend three days' leave shortly with his mother in Devon, so would I please have it on time. I said I would do my best and offered to take an extra-large dose of cascara, but he said hastily there was no need for that. Luckily, it did arrive on time and I was most relieved to have pleased Lionel on that score.

The confinement was deep in difficulties. It was a forceps delivery, and the baby was born with mild paralysis, and had to be injected with Vitamin K. For a whole day they were anxious for me too — I could not move my left side at all — but at last it passed off. They kept me a week longer than usual in hospital, however.

For two years I adored Elizabeth Jane. Matters with Lionel meantime went from bad to worse, however, and we fought like cat and dog. Nevertheless, it was a great shock to me when, one day, he came up to the nursery as I was putting Elizabeth down in her cot and after standing silently for a minute, asked if I would give him evidence for a divorce. I was furious — I knew he had been talking me over again with his mother, and no doubt this was her suggestion. All the same, a short time after this we separated and Elizabeth was placed in a residential nursery somewhere in the Home Counties. I have never seen her since. As I get older, the heartache of that parting seems to increase, and I would give anything to find her again, and my husband too. Just as soon as was legally possible after that, he got a divorce and the custody of Elizabeth, and I have no idea where they may be. I pray she escaped the kind of life and sufferings that came my way.

When I think about the past, as I can hardly fail to do — often — memories like these keep returning and fill me with a shattering feeling of guilt and remorse. I suppose it is one way I must pay for my past — I could hardly hope to have done so many awful things and be unscarred. Then again, I realise how much those days have taught me about people and living, and I am thankful to be so much stronger and more mature as a result.

At the time we parted, I was pregnant again. It was Lionel's child — during those two years, I had not played about at all with other men — but he wanted to know nothing about it or me. I had nowhere to go, and the only thing I could think of was to make my way down to his mother in Devon. She would not have me with her, however, so I took a room in a cheap boarding-house nearby. I had to pay two pounds for it, the whole of my weekly service allowance, and Lionel allowed me nothing above that. When he came down on leave, he stayed with his adoring mother and only came to visit me two or three times in the whole nine months, and then we had the most fearful rows.

Once, when I was about seven months pregnant, I telephoned him—he insisted that I only communicated with him by letter or telephone—and asked if we could talk things over. He suggested we should meet and go for a walk. He would not have me up at the house, and always chose some out-of-the-way alley if he had to meet me at all, so that his friends would not see us together. We took the coast road, along the cliffs. Suddenly, he linked his arm through mine—I was astonished, for he had not made such a friendly gesture in months. Then I feared that, as we were walking, he was slowly guiding me right to the edge of the cliff. I broke away and went round to his other side, remarking that I did not like being so near the edge. I have no evidence that there was anything in his mind. He told me a story of a dog which ran over that very cliff-edge and was killed. He never showed me another spark of affection.

I had no desire at all to have this other child in the circumstances, so I kept straining myself so that I would have a miscarriage. In a sense, I succeeded. The baby was almost a month overdue and had to be induced; I had a terrible labour and when I came round after, and asked the sister whether it was a boy or girl, she said evasively she would tell me later. I realised at once what that meant: the baby had been born dead. I was so distressed, I cried and cried. In amazement, the sister said, 'But surely, you wanted it this way!' How could I explain that I was crying for my whole unhappy marriage and the way things might have been if the baby had been born in happier circumstances.

After that, there was nothing to hold me. Although I had not bothered with other men during our marriage, it was a different matter now. I went back to London and Lionel easily got his divorce by checking on my activities there. Shortly afterwards, I heard he had got a transfer to the Fleet Air Arm—I can't think why he ever joined the Air Force in the first place. His heart was always with the sea and boats. His father had been in the Navy and Lionel had owned his own small yacht from an early age— even after we were married, he would go off sailing with Naval friends for weekend leaves.

All through our married life, he had allowed me very little money and I asked for very little. He once told me proudly that his bank manager had remarked how much more money there was in his account since his marriage. Lionel very rarely used any form of bad language, although there was plenty round him. There was just one four-letter word he would come out with on rare occasions when he was feeling mad with himself or with life. One day, I used the same word in front of him, for the very first time in my life. He twisted my arm and roughly pulled me to him and told me that if he ever heard it on my lips again, he would beat the living daylights out of me. I answered that he used it himself, but he said that was different: *I* was not to use it.

He had been to a good school and was always reading in his spare time — I can't think how he put up with my lack of education, for in those days, I was very ignorant and incompetent. My hardest form of reading was the *Daily Mirror*. I enjoyed things like sitting up in bed and polishing away at his buttons with Brasso while he was dressing to go out on early duty. He liked joining in the social round and here again, my lack of interest was a let-down. He drank a lot, but I never saw him the worse for it, and the last time I ever saw him was as we left the Divorce Court.

VII

AND SO I was in London again. In the lounge of a large West End hotel, I got into conversation with a Canadian Army officer. He gave me tea, then drinks, dinner and more drinks, and suggested we should go back to a flat belonging to a friend of his in a large block of flats in Regent's Park. By that time, I was in the mood for anything.

After our love-session was over, we were sitting drinking and talking, when the door opened and the Canadian's friend, a major, the owner of the flat, walked in. I was introduced and we all chatted for a little, then my officer said he had to catch a train back to camp. The major asked me to stay on: I spent the night with him, and then stayed on in the flat for many weeks, although he was far too old for me really — old enough to be my father. He had a wife and a grown-up son and daughter back in Canada. Moreover, he had another girl friend, a Canadian nurse, in this country. On the other hand, I was living in comfort for the first time since I came to England, and that was not to be sneezed at!

Each day we went off to our separate jobs. He was somewhere in the region of Trafalgar Square, and I had recently found work as a sort of assistant in the Civil Nursing Reserve. I finished my period of training, two weeks at a hospital down in Dulwich, and was posted to another near Barnet, part of which had been turned over to the care of servicemen. I was not qualified, but I could do what I was ordered in the way of washing patients, feeding them, making their beds and attending to minor dressings.

At the end of the day, it was wonderful to return to a luxurious flat, and spend the evening dining and dancing with the major. There was always plenty of good food, high spirits and a general sense of good living. A Canadian Army batman did the work in the flat — he spent most of his time in the small kitchen: I could never get beyond a formal good-morning with him. I think he resented the intrusion of yet another complication in the major's sex life.

69

In my job, I had days off, of course, and after I had been there some time, I was taking it easy on one such day in the flat, lying back in a deep armchair with my legs up, when my eyes rested on a large cabin trunk standing upright in a corner. I must have seen it before, but it had never struck me to wonder about it —now, with nothing to do, I suddenly became very interested in it. I crossed the room to investigate. It was firmly locked, but I knew the major had some keys in his desk. I found one which fitted, and the trunk was open. It was packed with the most elegant ladies' underclothes—the Canadian nurse's.

There was a photograph of her on the mantelpiece, years older than me but very good-looking and well-dressed. Here were her stacks of nylons, the most expensive bottles of perfume, and bras and panties in their dozens. To see all this in the middle of war-time and clothes-rationing was overwhelming. I sorted out a few things for myself, with a feeling of great luxury, and closed up the trunk. After a few days, however, I thought of another use for the clothes: I took some of the hundreds of pairs of nylons and sold them to other nurses at the hospital for five shillings a pair. (I *must* have been stupid: they were fetching about two pounds on the black market at the time!)

My raids on the trunk continued over the next weeks. One morning at hospital, the Matron called me into her office and reprimanded me for not wearing stockings with my uniform. I explained to her that I was wearing nylons, and she was most intrigued, as she had apparently never seen any before—I presented her with a pair for herself from my horde.

By now, there were, of course, very few articles left in the trunk and at last I began to wonder how long it would be before the major found out and what he would do. As well be hung for a sheep as a lamb: there was a small wardrobe also that was kept locked, and I turned my thoughts to getting that open too. I tried in vain all the keys I could find, and then luck took a hand. One afternoon when I was out shopping I passed a hardware shop and there in the window was the very type of key to fit the lock. I bought one.

Now the wardrobe opened, and, as I had guessed, it was also full of the nurse's clothes, all a girl could dream of, especially in war-time—at least a dozen model dresses, six suits, a fur coat, a dressing gown and heaven only knows how many pairs of shoes. I was stunned. The problem was never whether I should take them, but when and where I could wear them. Obviously I could not let the major or the batman, or even the other tenants at the flats, see me in them. Perhaps there was nothing to be done but to try on all these wonderful outfits and admire them in the glass, then slip them off again.

It was too great a temptation however—I longed to dress up like a Bond Street lady, even though if the major found out there would be hell to pay. Once or twice, when I knew there was no chance of his returning unexpectedly, I managed to put on one or other of the outfits on my day off and go out walking in the West End: it was a marvellous feeling, although I was terrified I would be found out. One morning, when the coast was clear, I put on a stunning suit. It was blue, most beautifully cut, and it had a very smart fur collar. I found myself shoes to match, nylons, gloves and a handbag, put on lashings of Paris perfume, and left the flat intending to walk down Regent Street for an hour or so's window shopping.

The batman had not yet arrived to do his daily chores, so I closed the flat door behind me and went down the stairs—I thought that was safer than the lift—and took a side corridor to the only exit unblocked by sand-bags. One of the flats had been taken over by the W.V.S. as an office, and looking out of it was a tenant who was a close friend, not only of the major, but also of his nurse. It was too late to retreat: I walked boldly past her, but though she did nothing, she looked me up and down accusingly as much as to say 'Those are not *your* clothes'.

Once I got round a corner, I began to run as quickly as the rather ill-fitting high heels would allow. I could hear her running behind me, but at last the main entrance was in sight and I was on the street. I went on running, but at last I saw over my shoulder that she was not following me, so I stopped and took breath. It had been a great shock, so I merely walked quietly round the block and back to the flat by another route. I had just got the clothes safely back in the wardrobe when the batman arrived.

The major was dead on time for lunch and unusually quiet through the meal. If I could have been sure that the tenant had got in touch with him, I would have packed my bag and fled, but I decided to chance it. On his way out again, the major said he might be home early and if so, we would have dinner in the restaurant and then go into the club for drinks and dancing, so *that* sounded all right. I threw myself on the bed and fell asleep.

Not for long, however. I woke to the crash-bang of doors, and there in front of me was the major. He pulled me from the bed and punched me and beat me, roaring accusations and abuse. I had no answer—it would have been no good. At last he collapsed into a chair, completely exhausted. I lay crying quietly on the bed, and when I next looked up, the major was going out. He told me not to move: he would be back shortly.

As soon as he was gone, I jumped up. Out in the kitchen, I could hear the batman washing up and clearing the dishes away. He must have heard every word and sound, but he did not come near me. I knew I must get away before the major came back—suppose he had gone to fetch the police? I pulled down my suitcase and threw all my clothes into it: there was no time for conventional packing. I put on a coat and headscarf, picked up the case and my purse and closed the door of the room quietly behind me. As I passed the kitchen door which, thank heavens, was closed, the batman was singing 'Bless 'em all!'

I took the lift down and luckily had it to myself. In the hall, I saw the major talking to the tenant who had seen me in the morning, but they did not notice me, and I managed to get straight into a taxi and drive away. No doubt but it was that woman who had split on me.

I never really liked the major—he was a mean-minded man—but he must have had to face the music when the nurse came on leave. I wonder how he explained to her where her nylons, perfume and underwear had gone—I hope she gave it him hot and strong!

. . .

Now, once more, I had no permanent roof over my head and I lived as best I could, in the only way I could, spending the nights with different men for somewhere to sleep. Sometimes I had money in my purse which they had given me, and then I would book in at a cheap hotel for the night and stay there on my own. Once a man I did not like the look of came and sat by me in a hotel foyer, and asked me to go to the pictures. I had nothing better to do, so I accepted. He took me back to the hotel and handed me a pound in an undercover way, telling me to go and book myself a room and then come back and tell him the number. The reception desk was a little out of his sight, so I walked towards it and right past it, out of the side door of the hotel. I jumped on a 15 bus which took me to the Strand, where I booked into a hotel room of my own.

At that time, I was what you would call a good-time girl. I went around with men because I enjoyed it. I picked them up in a hotel foyer or lounge. When they began eyeing me, I would smile. They usually beckoned me to their table, but I did not always go: more often, I unobtrusively indicated a place at mine and they would come over and ask if they could sit down. Then they bought me drinks and suggested dinner and perhaps dancing, and we would have a jolly good time. In return, all I expected was a place to sleep, and the odd present of nylons or dresses. If they gave me money, of course, that was better still.

But then I began to come across girls round the West End— some of them I saw at work and others I started talking to in the ladies' cloakrooms of the big hotels—and I realised I was silly. There was no reason why these men should get what they wanted for nothing. In future, they would have to pay for it —there were plenty ready and eager to do so. So I made a start on the professional life.

For some time, this was the way I existed, and because I had no room or flat of my own, we always spent the night in a hotel, signing in as husband and wife. I stayed in all types, from the posh ones such as the Dorchester, Park Lane, Cumberland, Claridge's, Berkeley, Ritz, Strand Palace, Regent Palace, Piccadilly and the Hyde Park, down to the flea-ridden doss-houses in Victoria. There were times during the war when it was difficult to get a room for one night, and that meant going about from place to place by taxi. We always got in somewhere—there was always someone who wanted your money and no questions asked. There was little difference in the rate of terms of the leading hotels and those that were nearer doss-house standard. My partners often paid up to four pounds for a rickety flea-ridden double room, but none of them ever quibbled about the price provided the room had a bed.

I never quite got over the embarrassment of asking for money, but I developed a regular routine. When their intentions became obvious, I used to say, 'Let's get things straight first. I'll lay my cards on the table: I shall expect a present in return.' In the early days, the present was about five pounds, and we usually ended up with breakfast. They always said it was all right by them, but as soon as we reached the bedroom, I said, 'Before we enjoy ourselves, let's get this money problem out of the way!' Only when matters were settled would I take my clothes off.

We usually had intercourse at least three times in the course of the night – there were occasions when I teamed up with record-breakers and received it six times, but these were rare. I enjoyed these sessions many times: a lot of my men were very handsome, and experienced lovers, and when that was the case we would both really go to town. At other times, when I was not much struck by my partner, I just chewed gum.

London was thronging with servicemen, mostly Americans, who seemed to have a hell of a lot of money. I liked the American servicemen – they knew what sex was and were very generous. I met a few Dutch Naval men, too, and they treated you as though you were a queen, so gentle, so loving and slow. I could not bear the Polish officers, they were *too* sexy for my liking. The other servicemen I had no time for were the Canadians – they were dead mean: if they could get something for nothing, they would, and if they did decide to pay you for your services, they wanted their money's worth. Mostly they tried to pay you in nylons, and that one leg at a time – they were a miserly lot.

English officers were at all times gentlemanly. You always felt at ease with them, not having to look at your handbag next morning to see if the money was still there, as I often found I had to do with the others. Incidentally, you may be surprised to learn that I never stole from my clients. From the time I became professional, the urge to steal seemed to have left me. You may think it strange, but I felt I was now at last making an honest living for myself.

I rarely worked on Sundays. Often I would slip into Westminster Cathedral on that day to hear the High Mass – the music was so beautiful and soothing. Later, when I was living near Shepherd Market, I would hear the Salvation Army band strike up and go out and join in all their hymns with a will. And on Christmas Eve, I never once missed the Midnight Mass – I would work until just beforehand, and try to persuade my last customer to come with me: they usually did. After that, I always went off somewhere to sleep on my own.

In between the sex, I had lots of fun, gay times, dancing mostly: I loved to dance and dance. As a child I would spend hours and hours in front of long mirrors dancing for the sheer

74

pleasure. I used to go to day-clubs, night-clubs or dinner- or tea-dances at hotels, if not with a man then on my own. I remember one early evening meeting an American Air Force pilot, and we danced until the early hours. That may not sound an unusual feat, but this man's whole back was encased in plaster of paris and the sweat was running from him. He had twenty-four hours' leave from hospital, and I was terrified he would collapse when he was with me. We had a wonderful evening, however, ending up with a sex session.

During this homeless period, I was able to manage for clothes and washing through the kindliness of the motherly souls in charge of the ladies' cloakroom at one of the big hotels. They listened to all my worries and troubles and gave me good advice as well. I would arrive at the cloakroom in the morning as soon as it opened, and before any other patrons came. I more or less stripped and had a jolly good wash and brushed my teeth. We took good care the hotel housekeeper did not catch me, or the attendants would have been in trouble, as a strip-wash was strictly against the rules of the hotel. The women kept my clothes in their little room and each day, I would go there to change into a different outfit. Of course, I tipped these attendants very well indeed, but they really were most kind to me.

There was one hotel for which I had a great affection. I used to lead a real cat and mouse life there: I was the mouse and the hotel manager and the house detective were the cats. I would often meet someone staying there who would ask me back—at a price—to his bedroom. At that time, most hotels were very strict on men taking girls who were not registered as their wives into their rooms, but on many occasions I dodged the watchers. When I had learnt the man's room number, we would part and I would allow him to go on upstairs while I perhaps went into the ladies' powder room to pass the time.

There were two routes by which I could get upstairs. I knew that the main foyer and lifts were strongly watched by the cats, so sometimes I would pass quickly through and down the stairs to the restaurant. There I would press for the lift, which as a rule was waiting empty on the ground floor. The liftman knew me and what I was up to. I would press five shillings into his hand and he would take me non-stop to whichever floor I wanted and then it was only a matter of dodging the chamber-maid.

75

My other route was to fly up the back staircase, and that was a killing business, running up perhaps seven flights of stairs. Sometimes I had to sit down at the top of one for a moment to get my breath back, but I dared not risk a second breath: I had to push on. It was quite a different matter coming down the back stairs afterwards. With my money safely in my purse and all the tension behind me, I felt a lot happier: I would go off and get myself a room for the night – if I did not team up with someone else who needed my attentions.

Once after such a session, I took a room for myself in the hotel, and thinking it was a pity to waste the chance of making some money, I went down into the foyer to pick someone up. I found a man in civilian clothes, very well-dressed, and he agreed to give me three pounds for what was called 'a short time'. We both went up in the lift together, a foolish thing to do, and as we were getting out of the lift on my floor, I thought he said something to the liftman, though as I was a little ahead, I could not be sure.

We entered my room and locked the door behind us. I took off my skirt and was about to take off the rest. He had taken off his jacket and his shoes, which he planted in the middle of the floor, unseen by me. All of a sudden, there was a loud bang on the door, a key put in the lock and a loud voice ordering me to open it. I threw on my skirt and told the man to hide behind a large deep chair, and then opened the door. In came the house detective and two hall porters. I protested that there was no one else in my room, but there in the middle of the floor stood the shoes as strong evidence. The man stepped forward with his jacket on – they had set me this trap and I had fallen right into it.

I was told to leave there and then. It was midnight, and I pleaded with them to allow me to stay until the following morning. They insisted, however, and to prove that they meant what they said, they called in two chambermaids to strip the bed and make it up for a new occupant. So I had to get out. The only redeeming part of this affair was that I had the three pounds still in my pocket – as usual, I had been wise enough to get that first. I expect the hotel thought it well worth the cost, for they were having a lot of trouble with girls like me.

The same thing happened to me at another hotel. The only difference was that the management burst in just as we were deep in the middle of intercourse, a very wrong time, very bad on the

76

nervous system. I had to leave once more, but I was luckier there: they allowed me to stay till morning.

At one time when rooms were short, some hotels would allow extra beds to be put into a room, for which they charged the full rate. Once there were four of us girls sharing one room, one on the bed proper, two on camp beds and the fourth on a mattress. We divided the blankets between us. Next morning the chamber-maid had a shock when she came in, on some pretext or other, and found us all sitting up eating grapefruit which an American Naval officer had given me.

All this time, I had had no place of my own, but one morning, while I was having coffee in a hotel lounge, I met Jacqueline. She was one of the girls and I had often spoken to her.

'I'm just off to look at a new flat down in Maida Vale,' she said. 'Would you like to come along with me?'

We set off. We were received by the housekeeper, who said that she had not just one small flat vacant, but two. When Jacqueline had chosen the one she wanted, I asked for the other, and I got it. It was my first fixed, permanent address and I was delighted. In fact, I was so delighted with having a flat of my own and what's more, a bed of my own, that the first thing I did was to go to bed and sleep for a solid twenty-four hours.

VIII

WHEN I first started the racket, you could always be sure of a pick-up in the big West End hotels, either in the lounge or the foyer, at any hour of the day or night. There have been times when I have counted up to forty girls, business girls. Wartime was the peak — afterwards you never seemed to find such vast numbers gathered together all at once. These hotel girls were on the whole a nice type. Most of them were hoping eventually to find a husband, or to save enough to buy a little business of their own or a place to retire to.

Many of them achieved their ambition, but I never learned to save until it was too late. I was no longer making the really big money then, and I was spending all I had in desperate attempts to find a way out of the life. In the early days, as soon as I had money, I spent it, not just on food and clothes and high rents but I was such an idiot, I would give it away to any Tom, Dick or Harry who needed it. Sometimes it was the other girls when they were in difficulties. Once, I remember, I fell in love with a ponce. He had some great scheme for running a syndicate and I was so much infatuated by him, I was quite prepared to go in with him, even though I had always sworn to keep my independence. I went and drew one hundred pounds from the Post Office, but when I met him in the street and tried to give it to him, he pushed it back at me roughly and refused to take it. He couldn't understand anyone being such a sucker, so he thought it must be some kind of police trap! I was heart-broken, and upset at having to carry so much money on me through the streets again. I tucked it down my chest, and I didn't know a minute's peace of mind until it was safely back in the Post Office.

I came to know some of the other girls quite well. Jacqueline who found me the flat was a blonde of about thirty-nine, a trained nurse from Clacton. She was always very well-groomed — most of her money went on clothes and furs. She was fond of her drink too, and was forever telling me about the nice man she hoped to marry one day—for some reason he would have to come from Scotland. Two things I remember in particular about her. In every spare minute she read detective stories: she had stacks of them in paperback and was always getting them out of her local lending library—and she was mad about heating. Her rooms, winter and summer, were like a furnace—I would have passed out, if it had been me. The large gas-fire would be turned up to the full, the windows tightly shut and steam pouring down them. No wonder that later on she suffered from chest trouble. Very few of her men friends seemed to return, either.

Then there was Maria. Out of all the girls I knew, she was the one who was really my friend. She was the sort of girl men would have looked twice at in any walk of life, tall, elegant, with very dark auburn hair. She had run away from her home up in Wales, where she had lived with an old aunt. She was very well-spoken, without a trace of a Welsh accent, and could converse on most subjects. She adored the clubs—night-clubs—and spent a lot of time there, but like me, I don't think she was all that interested in the racket itself, though she was a sexy type.

She was a great girl for falling head over heels in love. At one time, she fell deeply for a man who owned a large West End restaurant, but he was already married. Still, she became pregnant by him, which was a real disaster, for she had had so many abortions that she knew her health would not stand the shock of another and she would have to go through with it, her first live baby. Like most of us girls when we become pregnant, she carried on working right up to the last moment. I remember well going to see her at last, carrying a large bunch of flowers with me, in a private nursing-home somewhere in Swiss Cottage. She was so thrilled with the baby, and so sad at the prospect of having it taken away from her in a few days to be adopted. It was a heartbreak for her because she not only loved the baby but also the father—not that she received any return of her love. Where men were concerned, money was never the chief factor with Maria, as long as she had enough to meet her everyday expenses. When she loved, it was just for love—she was made that way. She had one very long romance with a singer in the night-clubs: he was everything to her. One strange thing about her: all during the war, she seemed to prefer the men who were in civilian clothes—you rarely found her with anyone from the Forces.

She was a casual type, too. I called on her once to have coffee and a chat in the morning, and found her on the telephone to one of her many admirers. I could hear a bath tap running. I sat and waited for her to finish talking—some fifteen minutes went by. I could still hear the tap, but Maria seemed oblivious to it. I got up from her settee and began to walk through her bedroom towards the bathroom, but I did not get very far: the water from the bath was flowing out to meet me! It was a shocking sight and we spent the next three or four hours mopping up: it took two days to dry out and she was very lucky it did not seep down through the ceiling to the flat below.

She had to watch her step very carefully in that flat, for it was in a very luxurious, expensive block. It was fortunate that there were two entrances to the flats, one of which came right out on Pall Mall. Another reason why she got away with taking men up and down was that she was well in with the day and night porters—she was a strange mixture: although she was so romantic, she would have intercourse with any Tom, Dick or Harry when she had been drinking.

A year or so after the war, she married a Polish Army officer —I should not think he knew much about her past, and certainly not about her baby. They went abroad for about three years before returning to settle down somewhere in this country—the social life abroad must just have suited her, for she was really in the racket for the good times it brought—the money enabled her to live at the standard she enjoyed. Of all the girls I knew, I liked her the very best—she was such good fun.

There were many more. There was Janneen, Irish like myself, who surprised me as we were passing the Jesuits' church in Farm Street during an air raid by saying: 'Let's go in and pray!' It was early on a winter's evening, and the church was almost dark except for the candles glowing on the stands by the statues. It seemed so friendly and safe after the streets, and so companionable to kneel side by side there. We stayed for half an hour, but churches closed early during war-time, and we could see a Jesuit waiting by the door to lock up, though he was too courteous to interrupt us. Reluctantly we got up and went back to the life that was waiting for us outside.

After that, I began to go more frequently to Mass in Westminster Cathedral—the ten-thirty daily Mass was a sung one and I had always loved the music. I would totter there, my eyes only half open sometimes, but gradually it became an almost daily habit with me, though of course, remaining of my own will in a state of sin, I did not make my communion. Churches were always a sort of haven to me, and I often went in even if they were not Roman Catholic, and sat down for a while to sort out my problems.

I noticed that in the Cathedral there was always a priest on duty in the confessional but that, at that time, was not for me either—I was not ripe or ready to shed my years of sin. It was not always the same priest, but I came to notice one particularly. Often, when no one was kneeling outside the box waiting to make their confession, he would walk softly and silently up and down the side-aisle reading his Office. Whenever I passed him, he always had a smile and whispered 'Good morning!' for me. I found out he was Father Michael Hollings.

It was many months before I summoned up courage to speak with him. I remember one dull morning in winter arriving in the Cathedral a little earlier than usual and going up to the Lady Chapel just in time to hear the tail-end of a Mass. I leaned up against one of the stone pillars and tried to take in as much as my fuddled mind would allow—I had been unable to sleep for the past thirty-six hours and only some two hours past had taken a dose of sleeping tablets.

I turned, and through the open partition-window of the confessional I could see Father Hollings. He seemed to give me a compassionate understanding smile and I was so grateful. I would have liked to have gone and spoken to him there and then: there were no people waiting for him. But I held back; I lacked the courage to make the first move. It was later, much later, that I ventured to talk to him and then he was so kind to me. Once, he gave me two of the books he had written—they were called *Hi You* and *Purple Times*. I loved those two books: they were so near to the mark of man's longing and loving of Christ.

After that, I often went round to the Cathedral clergy house to talk with him and at first I tried very hard to keep from him what I was. Somehow, however, I feel that from the very start, he must have had an idea of the life I was leading.

But I was talking of the girls I met on the racket. Several of them were Jewish. In particular, there was Rachel, a Cockney and about the most illiterate girl I ever came across. She could read—just—but she could write nothing beyond her name.

Nevertheless, men were fascinated by her – I have seen them sit spellbound at her sheer commonness – and she had several blue-blooded clients. She had been married twice and the break up of her first marriage had been a great blow to her. She had a little girl who was mentally defective, but she could never be brought to see it. Her mother looked after him for her.

I shared a flat with her for a few months, very large, with about six rooms, in Madder Street near Grosvenor Square. We each had our own bed-sitting room and shared the vast kitchen and bathroom. The other rooms were empty, not a stick of furniture in them. At weekends we would give the flat a real good cleaning, including the long hallway. It was always part of my job to clean the kitchen: it had old-fashioned dressers with lots of shelves to scrub – the floor alone took me nearly an hour. It was quite a sight to see the two of us hard at work, me with just a pair of panties and a sweater, scrubbing away, and Rachel, stark naked, waxing the floor unconcernedly just as though she were fully dressed.

While I was living with Rachel, I would go along every morning to Berwick Market in Soho to get the day's shopping. I went out in old clothes, so that I wouldn't be recognised. I met the same girls I would meet at night again in Shepherd Market and round about, and we would laugh and gossip – the stall-keepers all knew us: it was great fun. Sometimes I would arrive back with oranges, bananas and fresh eggs. It was ration time and they were all in the region of ten shillings a dozen, but if you had the money and the contacts, you could find them, and on the whole we lived very well at the flat. Sometimes I would do the cooking when I got back. In all my life I have never eaten so much smoked haddock as I did with Rachel – it seemed always to be smoked haddock or smoked kippers, but then, of course, meat was rationed too.

Ingrid – now there was a girl who was different from the rest. She was a Canadian doctor's daughter, very well-spoken and intelligent, and she was what you would call a one-man girl. She had been married, but her husband had gone off and left her. She was happiest if she could find a man who would put a roof over her head and give her plenty to drink: she would stay with him for months on end. She was the most untidy, slovenly girl I ever met, however – I have known her go in to the Savoy Hotel with her hair still in curlers.

Then there was Naomi. When I first met her, she had just gone through a divorce. She was Jewish too, quiet and a nice girl. She had sole custody of her two sons and spent every penny she earned on the streets to keep them at a very expensive boarding school. She was obsessed by spiritualism, and implicitly believed what the spirits told her, particularly about money. Somehow, they were always promising her a large sum for a certain day, and she would come home from a seance and tell you excitedly all about it. When the day arrived without the money, she would be very upset. She had to have all her teeth out, and for some months she was on the job without any teeth at all, but it seemed to make no difference! Poor Naomi, she ended in a mental home.

And there was Dawn. When I first met her she was little more than seventeen, with wonderful long red hair. She was very popular with the Americans, and she eventually married an American officer. The reason that came about was that one night she met him in Piccadilly and took him back to her room, and they were just finishing intercourse when the wrong time of the month happened to her. She was embarrassed by this, and put on an act of not knowing what could be the matter, as her monthly period was not due. That led him to believe she had been a virgin until then—he fell for that and he fell for her, and they married and went to live in America.

On the whole, prostitutes are not criminal types. Most of them work for themselves and not to keep a ponce, and they were very law-abiding, at least round the West End. I have met some exceptions, however, and Beryl was one. She was clever and intensely wicked, and always to be found in the company of coloured men as criminal as herself. She first came into my life one evening when I was walking round Curzon Street with a problem on my mind. I was pregnant and needed to have an abortion: it would be my fourth, but the woman I usually went to was not available. Beryl was also walking round Curzon Street, also on the racket, and we got talking. She knew someone who would be prepared to do an abortion—at a price, but I was quite prepared to pay.

She invited me round to her flat nearby for a cup of tea, and over it, she offered me the use of the flat for a number of months, if for every man I took into it, I would pay her two pounds. It was very convenient for me at that time, and it was a really lovely flat, but anyone who knows about such matters will realise that for two girls to carry on prostitution in one flat is against the law, for the flat then counts as a brothel. Beryl was obviously aware of the risk—she was years older than me and had been on the racket far longer. She wanted easy money, and it meant she would not have to do any hustling herself: I was at that time young and attractive, and I was in and out of that flat from late afternoon until after midnight, making as much as a hundred pounds a week—that and my time in Hertford Street were really my peak period: it was all in and out work, at three to five pounds a time, though, of course, there was Beryl's rake-off and the Hertford Street rent was twenty guineas a week.

It was too good to last—after some months Beryl was arrested and charged with running a brothel. Luckily I was not in the flat the night the police arrived. I had gone back to my own small flat, which at that period was in South Norwood. On the morning of the court case, I was at the hairdressers: I was planning to go over to Dublin for a week's rest in a nursing home as I was feeling rather strained and tired. My head was down in the washbasin, when I was called to the telephone: one minute more and my hair would have been drenched with water. It was Beryl, phoning from Marlbro Street in what sounded like great distress. She had been fined forty pounds and unless she could pay it immediately, she was going to be taken to Holloway Prison for three months. Would I, she pleaded, come along and help her out with the money? (I was not to know that she already knew the inside of Holloway only too well).

I felt sorry for Beryl. If I gave up my plans for the rest in Dublin, I would just about have enough to get her free. There seemed nothing else to be done: I abandoned my hair appointment, rushed out for a taxi and drove to Bow Street. Beryl was sitting in a cell. I paid her fine and she was released. As we walked out together, she grabbed the receipt from my hand and tore it fiercely into tiny pieces. She scattered them along the pavement as we went, but she gave me no word of thanks; in fact, for some reason, she seemed absolutely mad with me. We went back to her flat, where several of her friends were gathered to hear the outcome of the case. Then she turned on me and abused me, claiming the whole police raid was my fault—my fault, yet, as I said, I had left her some time before, and she had had other girls working for her since! It was so unjust. And then she struck

84

me across the face. I began to see what a dangerous woman she could be.

'Look, Beryl,' I said, 'if I never see my forty pounds again, O.K. — I don't mind the money. But I don't ever want to see you again.'

She made another rush at me, but one of her friends held her back and I made my escape. Outside, I ran into two policemen, and complained bitterly about what Beryl had done.

'Why don't you take out a summons against her?' they said, so I went back with them to the station, and the upshot was that Beryl was bound over to keep the peace. She got even with me soon after, however, for when I had a flat in Mount Street, she went and told the landlady I was on the racket, and I was out in the street in no time. I kept as far away from Beryl after that as I could.

There were other girls I cannot forget — some ended up like Naomi in mental hospitals, because they could not stand the strain of the life. One or two were there because they had been beaten unconscious by men. A handful died from back street abortions, and some I knew were murdered. It was a life full of dangers.

IX

BUT WE must return to the time that I got my first flat, in
Maida Vale. I had not been there long when I discovered that I
was pregnant — in fact, I was already a few months gone. At that
time, I was not all that wise about matters of contraception, and
that was the reason for the condition I found myself in.

I was not unduly worried — there was some time to go yet: I
could easily fall downstairs or something, so I made no plans.
Of course, I began to try to find someone to get me out of it,
but I seemed quite unable to make the right contacts.

One afternoon, I walked down one side of Harley Street and
up the other, ringing every other doorbell and asking to see
whatever doctor's name was on the brass plate. The reception-
ists would ask my name, and I told them I had no appointment
but had called on chance. They thought it strange, but I was
ushered into several doctors' consulting rooms. *They* must
have thought it even stranger, when I explained that I wanted
them to carry out an abortion on me.

One doctor, telling me like the rest that he could not help me,
added that when my pregnancy was over, he would be only too
glad for me to call on him again, and he would fit me out with
a proper contraceptive. He suggested I should recommend him
to my friends as well. Another, at one of the last doorbells I
rang, refused to perform my request, but offered to make arrangements for me to have the baby in a nursing home where they would
see to getting it adopted. I thought that if I could get no one
to do the abortion, this might be the next best thing. Incidentally,
this last doctor charged me three guineas for telling me this —
the others had not charged me a penny. He also warned me the
nursing home fees would be fifty pounds, but I was prepared to
save hard to collect that.

After this Harley Street affair, I carried on as usual until I
was seven months pregnant. By then, I was very tired: after all,
I was having intercourse perhaps two or three times a night, and

was not getting an adequate diet to cope with the strain. I really did not care what happened to me, when at last I found someone to do an abortion, and although so far on in pregnancy it was very dangerous, not only for the child but for me, I was quite willing to die if necessary.

I had been standing one evening in a hotel entrance, when across the way I noticed another pregnant girl, and although we did not know each other, we smiled. Then she crossed over to where I was standing, and after some moments' conversation, we began to talk of our condition. When she told me she knew someone who would carry out an abortion, I was delighted, especially as the fee was only twenty pounds and I had already saved that amount. We arranged to meet the very next morning in the ladies' waiting room at Waterloo Station at twelve o'clock, and I was to have the twenty pounds ready to hand over to the contact, who would then make arrangements for the abortion.

I made my way to that ladies' waiting room with the feeling that the girl would not turn up, but I had only been there five minutes when she arrived. I began to feel more hopeful. She asked if I had the money, and I told her it was safely tucked away down my chest. We had met at Waterloo because the contact, a shopkeeper, lived at Kingston, so now we caught a train there. We found his chemist's shop in a side-alley. It was very respectable-looking, and so was the contact. He was about forty-five and wore glasses – you could have seen hundreds like him any day behind a chemist's counter.

It was soon settled – the following Friday, a woman would call at my address to do the operation. I handed over the twenty pounds and walked out of the shop, and then turned back and asked the shopkeeper for a receipt: after all, it was a lot of money. He obligingly scribbled a more or less illegible note for me – at least it was something to hold on to, if the whole thing turned out to be a confidence trick.

The other girl, whose name was Eileen, very kindly offered to come along to my flat on the Friday and stay with me during the operation: I was very grateful to her, and we arranged to meet that day for lunch. I remember that meal so well – we were in some kind of a working men's café, and it was terrible: the cabbage was nothing but water.

Back at the flat, we waited for the midwife. I got everything ready, two kettles of boiled water, packs of cotton wool and so

87

on, but after hours of waiting in suspense, drinking endless cups of tea and smoking cigarette after cigarette, we began to wonder if I had not been taken for a ride.

Next day I rang up the contact and asked why the woman had not turned up. He assured me there must have been some misunderstanding and said she would definitely be there the next Friday. So the following week again saw Eileen and myself sitting in the flat waiting for her. I was now worried, and anxious to get the whole affair over and done with. Just to play safe and not tempt my luck, I did not boil the water beforehand.

The appointed time was two o'clock in the afternoon, but it must have been nearer four when at last the woman put in an appearance, and as I had long given up hope, I was just over-joyed to see her. She was big, jolly and motherly, but one can never judge character by appearance. When she saw how big my pregnancy was, she seemed a little taken aback. When I told her I was seven months gone, she said that as a rule she only did pregnancies up to three months — beyond that, it was a bit risky for her. I got upset when she said that, as I was afraid that after all she was not going to carry out what she had come to do, but she quickly assured me she would go ahead. She then offered to do Eileen at the same visit if she had twenty pounds on her.

I put my foot down firmly at this, whether or not Eileen had the money. There were not, I said, going to be two abortions at the same time in *my* flat, and that was that. Funnily enough, Eileen did not seem in the slightest way worried about her own condition, anyway. She just said all the time that everything would work out. Perhaps it was partly the money — I gave her five pounds afterwards for looking after me, and I only wish I could have afforded to let her have the whole twenty she would need.

Now it was time for the operation. The midwife took off her coat and drank the cup of tea we offered her. She made no attempt to boil the water to sterilise it: she just used ordinary tap-water. All was now set. Just as she was about to insert the syringe, she said:

'Now remember, if you feel the slightest pain, call out and tell me.'

Lying on top of the bed in only my pyjama top, I was naturally rather nervous — I would have been much more so if I had realised the terrific risk I was taking, but I was very young and inexperienced. The woman was well in the middle of her job when I cried out, and then was violently sick and began to have diarrhoea. I was in a very bad way, and suffering severely from shock.

When the midwife saw my condition, she quickly packed her bags, threw on her coat and left. I have never seen anyone rush away so fast. Thank heavens, Eileen was there to do what she could for me. The bed was one hell of a mess and I was stone cold. The blankets seemed no use to me, so somehow, I don't know quite how, I got off the bed and dragged myself along the floor to the large gas fire. Eileen turned it up to its full height and I lay down as close to it as I could get. That blessed heat was the most wonderful thing that ever happened to me. I believe it saved my life.

I still felt very ill, so I got into the bed while Eileen made me a hot drink. All this time she had been urging me to call a doctor, but I told her to wait a little longer — I wanted the abortion to be so complete that no doctor could save it. It seemed rather stupid to fail at this stage when I had paid good money to go through with it.

After another hour or so, Eileen went off to the public call box, armed with a load of pennies, to call a doctor. She had great difficulty in getting one to come out so late in the evening. They refused to come because I was not on their panel. In the end, one doctor agreed to come when she said I would be his private patient.

He arrived very quickly, and his well-trained eye must have realised my serious condition. He asked me how the abortion had happened and I told him some old story of having fallen down the stairs, but I am afraid he was too experienced to believe that tale. I must say he was extremely kind. My temperature was sky-high, so he went himself to a telephone and made arrangements for me to be taken to hospital by ambulance. The ambulance men carried me downstairs on a stretcher — it was lucky that during all this commotion the housekeeper and the other tenants were out — and took me to Paddington General Hospital. Eileen was a great help, switching the lights off and locking the flat door behind us. She even came as far as the hospital with me.

Within an hour of my arrival, the abortion was complete, but before this I had to go through great pain and discomfort.

For a few days, they kept me under special observation, because my life was in danger, but I came through.

The ward I was in was a very long one, and practically every case was an abortion. It was known among the patients affectionately as the Piccadilly Ward, for obvious reasons. My operation left me very weak, but after some weeks of extra rest and food, I was back to the old life again. I often wonder what became of Eileen, though — she came and visited me once in hospital, but she left me no address, and I never saw her again.

I must have had about eight more abortions after this, carried out by all kinds of people, from back street abortionists like that midwife to Harley Street doctors whose fees were a hundred guineas. Give me the Harley Street man every time, for you felt quite safe in his skilled hands, and if you had to pay a higher fee, he was taking a tremendous risk. My friend Maria had the record number of twelve abortions, but always by the same Polish doctor — once, when he had operated on her, she became so ill that he had to keep her in his surgery for two days, and for that time he cancelled all his other appointments to look after her.

I learnt one hard lesson. Once when I was pregnant, I found it difficult at the start to get hold of an abortionist, so I thought I would carry it out myself with knitting needles and things. I was lying on the hearthrug at the time, and my eye rested on my bedside lamp, which had a very small light bulb. I anointed myself with lots of Vaseline and managed to get that bulb into my vagina and switched on the current. It was an idiotic thing to do: the bulb could have smashed inside me, or I could have been electrocuted. The heat became too much to bear, so I started to pull on the flex gently to get the bulb out: it was terribly difficult to do, and I had to use nearly a whole jar of Vaseline.

An hour or so later, I began to feel very ill. I got myself to St. George's Hospital, to the casualty department. They examined me and took my temperature — it was very high, so they kept me in a few days for observation. They seemed baffled by the case and, of course, I never told them what I had done. It was no use, however — I left the hospital still pregnant, and had to have a more conventional abortion later.

Another thing I learnt was never to get mixed up in another person's abortion. I was out walking in Shepherd Market one day when a gentleman fell into step beside me. I began putting my usual suggestions to him, but he cut me short — that was not what he wanted, he said: he was looking for someone to perform an abortion. Could I help him? We went to have a drink and talk it over. Under the table he handed me five pounds, promising me twenty more if I found him someone. I managed to arrange it, his girl friend arrived in London, and I put her up in my flat.

The next day, we took a bus over to Maida Vale to find the woman who was to perform the operation. We rang the doorbell once, twice, three times, but there was no reply. We went and had a cup of tea in a nearby café and after that tried again. Still no reply.

The hall door was glass, and it occurred to me that if the woman had seen two figures waiting, she might have thought we were policewomen. The next time, I quickly pressed the bell then sat down on the doorstep and began to play with a black cat which was sunning itself there. The door opened, and there was the woman herself. It did not need much intelligence to see that she was rather the worse for drink.

We went upstairs to her flat and sat and talked: I wondered how anyone as drunk as she was would be able to carry out such a serious operation. She did it, however, quite well—perhaps she needed Dutch courage. I gave her twenty pounds, the girl lay down on the bed and that was that: it was all over. We went back to my flat and by night-time the abortion was complete.

Later, however, I began to consider the risk I had run. Supposing it had not been successful, and the girl had died in my flat—everything would have pointed to my having done the operation myself—to begin with, they would have found the douches I kept for my own use. The woman would have got clean away with it, and I would have had a terrible job to prove my innocence.

I must tell you one other story of an abortion, though it makes me ill to think of it again. At one stage, when I had a flat off Sloane Street, I had a maid who came in daily from nine to twelve to do the cleaning. One day, as she gave me my breakfast-tray in bed, she told me that the day before, she had been helping a woman carry out an abortion on a young girl who was about six months pregnant. A few hours later, the baby was born alive; it started to cry and they put the new-born baby on the open fire. This is no story I am telling you. It is dead fact and when she told me, I was sick. I pushed away my tray and told that maid to get out and never, never, never come near me again. She was a murderer—I told her so. I had no qualms of conscience where an unborn baby in the womb is concerned, but once it is born and alive, that was a very different matter.

.   .   .

One evening towards the end of the war, a girl I knew came along and said she had just been to St. Thomas's Hospital for a venereal disease test, and she thought all the other girls ought to go. It seemed a good idea. I was in for a shock, however, for though I had no external symptoms, the test showed that I had syphilis. If the doctor had said I had cancer, the shock could not have been greater. I left the hospital in a daze—I have no idea how I got back to my flat.

For a whole eighteen months, I attended each week for the good old-fashioned treatment of arsenic and bismuth. Some of the others gave up before they were cured (Ingrid, I heard, is now in an advanced stage of the disease)—it was a long time. It was still the most reliable form of treatment, however, except for penicillin, which at that time was kept chiefly for the armed forces. The doctors and sisters were kindness itself. They were elderly and treated me like their child. Most of the other girls attending the clinic were ones I knew, so that it was more like attending a club. At last I was discharged—to this day I maintain there was a mistake in my Wasserman test! I always went regularly for tests after that, however, although I never again contracted the disease.

At one time, I went every three months, and at last the doctor at the clinic said, 'Tell me—not that we are not glad to see you at any time—but just as a matter of interest, why do you come so often?'

I was not going to tell him outright I was on the racket, so I said: 'Well, doctor—I do take chances with my boy friends.'

He smiled. 'You seem pretty intelligent to me,' he said. 'You would know the symptoms by now—swelling in the groin or armpits, and a rash without an itch. A check-up once a year should be quite enough, provided you promise to come in immediately if you notice anything wrong.'

At times, he and I had long discussions on venereal disease and its dangers—I am very grateful to him, for I learned a lot that way.

It was in a sense through my treatment for V.D. that I found again the only member of my family who cared for me later in life. I was travelling to Ireland, and I knew I was to stay with one of the family, though I was not told which. On the way, as a result of my treatment, I developed jaundice, and though I did not realise it until I took a bath later, turned bright yellow. My sister, Pauline, who was waiting for me in the crowd at the disembarkation point turned to her husband and indicating me, said, 'What a pathetic girl that is over there!' Her husband looked harder, and much shocked at what he saw, told her, 'That's Maureen.' From then on, these two took me to their hearts.

There were other health hazards to my job — one of them was body lice, or crabs, as they are generally called. They dig themselves into the parts of the body where there is a patch of hair, the eyebrows, under the arm-pit — but their main port of call is the lower part of the body. As far as I know they are not found on the head. They are passed on by contact. When they first hatch, they are difficult to see, but they grow to a size of a tenth of an inch.

I once caught them, and the itch was terrible. Luckily, there is a special liniment made up by chemists which soon kills them — before I heard about that, however, I had to try to dig them out painfully with nail scissors.

I met a man once in the West End who agreed to come home with me for business. We were lying on top of the bed playing around, and because I had learnt to be fastidious over cleanliness, I was secretly making a careful survey of his body. When I looked down at the lower part of his anatomy, he was just crawling with crabs. I was wild: I jumped off the bed and shouted at him to get up, get dressed and get out.

He looked at me as though I had gone crazy. I told him in no uncertain terms what I thought of him. 'And another thing,' I shouted angrily, 'don't ask for your money back! And if you want a girl again, don't look for one in Mayfair but take a journey into Hyde Park: they're not particular there.'

It was very rare, however, that I came across men of that type, for I had my own ways of choosing men. I was not a public convenience for every Tom, Dick and Harry.

X

WHEN I was on the game I always dressed well — well-cut suits from Harrods or Simpsons, and good shoes, with heels of only medium height. I had some beautiful fur coats too, for winter time, but they are long since gone. I would walk up and down, and when I saw a likely customer, I smiled at him. If he smiled back, I would fall in beside him and greet him as if we knew one another, or say 'Hello!' as I passed, and hurry round a corner so that he could follow me: this was for the benefit of the police, who were always on the look-out, even more particularly after the passing of the Street Offences Act in 1960. (It was much safer to stand about in Shepherd Market, as there were so many girls there that the alarm was easily raised if the police were sighted.) Then I asked my customer if he would like to come home with me and if (say) five pounds was all right. If we were some distance away, we took a taxi back, and that was it.

I had my own ways of choosing my men. I would note the clothes they were wearing, their shoes — whether they were good leather, and well-polished — shoes are a very important clue to a man. If when I accosted them I saw their hands and finger-nails were dirty, I made some excuse and walked away. To me, personal hygiene was very important, and I took as few chances as I could. I was never without rubber contraceptives, and most men would not dream of having intercourse without one. I used to buy them from a cut-price shop a gross at a time: they worked out cheaper that way. Occasionally I was in a fix when a man refused to wear a rubber, and I did not want to have him demand his money back and leave the flat. At such times, I would take a large swab of cotton wool and insert it inside me when he was not looking — it did not help the enjoyment but it was as well to be careful.

Some of my men friends made very strange requests. It is often only women such as I was who are prepared to take seriously these odd ideas some men have. Many of these men are married. If only they had had understanding wives, they would not have needed to find their way to my flat. John always arrived by car carrying what looked like an ordinary brief case, but inside it was a complete nanny outfit: softly starched white apron, a nurse's white veil, baby's napkin, safety pins, Johnson's baby powder and rubber baby pants. I had to dress up as the nanny and then, when John had undressed, I had to bath him, shake plenty of baby powder over him, put on his nappy and rubber pants. Then, while I was cuddling and kissing him and perhaps crooning some old nursery rhyme, he would reach his climax. That was all he wanted.

Many of the men in my life have wanted to dress up in my underclothes and wear lashings of my make-up on their faces — this type seems much commoner nowadays. I was amazed at the number of them who walked round town wearing ladies' underwear under their everyday suits; bras, girdles, frilly panties and nylon stockings. I sometimes pleaded with them to think of the embarrassment they would cause if they were involved in some sort of street accident.

Tim was another who liked his sex in a strange way. He would come to my flat putting on an act that he was constipated and needed to be given an enema, just as some attractive nurse must once have given him one in hospital. I would get out my syringe and with some warm water and Dettol and soft green soap give him his enema. No contact with me whatever, but that was how he achieved a climax.

Nothing surprises me now but you would be shocked if I were to tell you even half. Some have a strange liking for the feel of rubber or nylon and like one or both of us to be naked except for a mackintosh. I found these rubber and nylon sessions were so very cold! I once met a man on a winter's evening when it was pouring with rain and there was quite a gale blowing: he wanted me to go up on Hampstead Heath with him, take off all my clothes, put on a rubber mac and make love in the open. Needless to say, I did not go — it would have been asking for trouble in a big way: he could have driven off with all my clothes, or far worse.

Then I would get the men who wanted me to beat and torture them or even wanted to do it to me. I never liked that sort of sex play, for I am by nature cuddly and affectionate, and anyway, I feel life has treated me harshly enough without my having

95

to put up willingly with that sort of thing. When I first went on the racket, I often met men like that. One paid me well to beat him and kept repeating 'Harder! Harder! Draw blood!' as each stroke of the whip he had brought along with him fell on his bare bottom. I felt so sick that at last I threw the whip at him and told him I could not go on.

The most revolting way men wanted to have their sex with me was by the rectum. Even now, to write of this revolts me and turns me sick with a sort of fear. Men who were the worse for drink I would not bother with, either. I liked men to know what they were doing. Once a man in a parked car in Berkeley Square beckoned me over, and I realised as I got in beside him he was very drunk—I thought he might sober up if I kept him there talking. When he seemed a little better we drove to my flat —he gave me ten pounds in one-pound notes. After an hour, we were still lying on top of the bed, having got nowhere. He was incapable from drink and all my methods and techniques had run out. He pleaded with me to get another girl, so being some-what desperate myself, I agreed: I felt rather sorry for him! But though the other girl and I tried as hard as we could, he was just not capable. He offered me another twenty pounds not to give up, but I told him that even if he offered a hundred, I could not go on—it was too much of a nervous strain. So I helped him dress and saw him safely back to his car.

I was walking along Piccadilly one late evening, when I met another man who seemed to have had a fair amount to drink. I was rather short of money, so I threw caution to the winds and took him back home. We both started to undress—yes, I must have been very tired, for usually I never undressed until I had received my present. He was standing over by the fire just taking off his vest when I asked him for the money. We had agreed that he would give me five pounds for a couple of hours. He went over to his wallet and fetched out two single pound notes.

I told him that was not enough—on Piccadilly we had agreed to five pounds. He crumpled the notes and threw them on the bed, then pushed me back on top of them and pressed firmly on my neck, intending to strangle me. I thought my end was coming, and I remember thinking how it would upset my self-righteous brothers and sisters when it was reported in the papers and they found out how I had been living.

The man was talking loudly: 'Baby,' he said, 'you have been

asking for this all your life and now you are going to get it.'

I managed to croak the word 'Water!' and, to my surprise, he released the pressure for a moment. As he had been drinking, I suppose the word perhaps appealed to him. He looked at me and I suppose realised what he had nearly done. He stood up straight. 'Don't move!' he said. 'I'll get you some.' I waited till he was in the bathroom, then like a flash I leapt off the bed, grabbed my flat keys and ran out in the nude. I rang the bell of the flat below: luckily the girl who lived there was in. I explained hastily and she threw her coat round me so that I could dash out to the public telephone box and ring the police.

I waited in the call box until the police arrived—fortunately it was very quick. I went back to the house with them and as we were going up the stairs, there was this man coming down, with my radio under his arm. He was not charged, however— it was only my word against him, and there were too few bruises for evidence. He had the cheek to ask me for his money back as the police were escorting him out, but they only said, 'Sorry! According to the law, you made a contract with this lady and you are not entitled to take it back.'

Although I had quite a number of convictions for prostitution I never bore the police any grudge—they were only doing their job. We all had to take our turn at coming before the magistrate, but they were very fair. They would come up to you —always uniformed men, of course, for if they had worn plain clothes, we could have claimed they had been picking us up in the way of business—and say, 'Come on, Myrtle—or Rita— your turn today!' They would take you along to the West End Central station, where the station sergeant took your particulars, and if he knew you, you could walk out again, but you had to promise to be at Bow Street next morning at ten.

You would find a whole group of old friends waiting there. A friendly police matron would take a roll-call, and we would chat away to the policemen and smoke with them until ten-thirty, when we went in to the magistrate one by one. The fine was two pounds, but if any of the girls had drunk away the money or were in for being drunk and disorderly and could not pay, we would whip round for them, and sometimes even add the price of a meal.

I have never got used to the ordeal of standing up before a magistrate, however, and I felt it much more as I got older. The whole court routine is only a matter of seconds, but it feels like a lifetime. I could not get used to being labelled 'a common prostitute', either.

To go back to my men. They were not all odd: many of them were well-educated and very courteous. I did not always 'pick them up' in the traditional way, either. When I had a flat in Mount Street, I used to follow the same route most evenings, a slow saunter round the block and back. I often met an ex-Army officer who had his town house somewhere in the neighbourhood, and he began to pass the time of day with me when we met. It was obvious to him what my profession was, but he was always most polite and rather fatherly in his manner. Whenever I saw him out with his wife, I always turned the corner or crossed the road, so as not to embarrass them, but if ever I did have to pass them both, she always gave me a smile too and a 'Good evening'.

One cold winter's night, I was slowly walking backwards and forwards and stopped for a moment to look around me just outside their house, when the front door opened and the butler beckoned me inside. (We had often had a chat out shopping in Berwick Market—I am pretty sure he was a homosexual.) He made me sit down in the hall and told me to wait. He came back carrying a silver tray with a wineglass on it and a bottle of brandy. I looked at him in amazement.

'With the Master's compliments,' he said.

Not long after, this gentleman asked me to help him. He had a young ex-Harrovian nephew who was about to get married, but knew nothing about the opposite sex—would I undertake to teach him the facts of life? He paid for it all discreetly beforehand, then introduced me to his nephew, who came to see me on several occasions, always bringing a bottle of Scotch with him. Believe me, he needed quite a few lessons in the art of sex, as he was very raw! I hope it helped to make his married life a good deal more successful than it would have been.

I have also been asked to act as co-respondent in many divorce cases, some of them famous, usually with the consent of both parties. This involved staying a night or two at one of the leading West End hotels. To make sure the chambermaids and floor waiters did not forget us, we spilt tea or coffee over the bedclothes, and tipped rather too heavily. Only once, however, did I have to appear in the Courts: usually the cases were undisputed.

I mentioned the butler—often when I was out on my rounds, I would come across the male prostitutes, and sometimes would talk with some of them. They were an odd lot: I could never really understand them.

Once a diplomat at one of the foreign Embassies, who was living in the same block of flats as I was, used to take me out to dinner and the theatre. He gave me presents of nylons and perfume and invited me to parties at his flat, but never once did he make the usual sexual advances to me. Then one evening when I was off to a club, he said to me, 'Maureen, find me a nice young boy, will you?'

I felt sorry for him, and for a while, I found him a succession of these young male prostitutes—he was rather fussy, and some of them he did not like, and it was rather difficult to find just the right ones. It ended when one of them stole a valuable watch from him: he could not go to the police, for fear the matter came to the ears of his Embassy. I told him then and there that it ought to be a lesson to him, and that I was finding him no more boys, young or old. We remained friends, surprisingly, but I took good care never to get involved again.

The so-called 'easy life' was not all roses—it was very hard on the nervous system and very tiring. I had to be girl friend, wife, mother, mistress, lover, nurse, besides something of a psychiatrist as well! Like the large commercial firms, the aim of my business had to be to please the customer—if he was not satisfied, he would not return. It was a very unsafe, lonely kind of life, however. Men came into my life, made love to me, told me they loved me and would be sure to return, but many never did. I gave them real love and affection, for those moments often meant something to me—I craved affection so much—but it was not so for them. Men like change in everything, not least their women.

I knew of no other way to earn my living, however—I had no training for any other kind of job, and I had got used to living like this. Consequently, I and many like me were hard hit in 1960 when the Street Offences Act came in. It was the older ones who felt it most: you can't teach an old dog new tricks. I agree that vice on the streets had got out of control, but to send us girls to prison, as happened under the new Act, was no answer. The doors of the prison and of the lunatic asylum are always open —never a 'House Full' sign: a kindly gesture on the part of society for those it can no longer cope with, who themselves do not know how to cope with life! I heard the other day that one of my old friends had died from an overdose. She had come before the courts after her third warning under the Act. She was fined twenty-five pounds, but she had not got so much and they sent her to Holloway. She could not stand it—she took her own life.

XI

IT WAS not a matter of age—you could go on until you dropped, though, of course, the younger girls had the advantage of their looks. It was the mental and physical strain which made girls give up or go mad or kill themselves. Many a time I tried to get out of the life—priests have called me a coward; I had only to be firm and take the step, but it was not that. You cannot reform an older prostitute just by words, and even less by condescendingly offering her charity: like other people, prostitutes have their pride. Many have come originally from good homes and are even extra sensitive and independent. There must be something practical to offer as an alternative, something to work and live for. I no longer cared about the clubs—they seemed an empty way of life to me by then, and they have changed anyway from what they were—but everyone needs sufficient money to live at a reasonable standard. On the other hand, after such a life, I am not going to say that girls like me will be normal and able to fit into an ordinary job: for one thing they will be so tired, and need long rest at first before they can manage the usual nine-to-five routine.

Not all prostitutes want to change their way of life—all right. But for those who do, there ought to be *some* way to go about it which does not involve losing their self-respect. For instance, since I began I had always had a flat of my own, except for the brief period I shared Rachel's. I love to listen to my radio and keep up with events. I like to read—to use my mind instead of my body. I crave security, a roof over my head, and above all, love and affection. Since the Street Offences Act came in especially, I tried more than once to get away, but some of the alternatives I was offered were laughable, though they were not all bad alternatives, or I would not be where I am today.

With the exception of my sister Pauline, none of my family knew or cared how I was existing over in England: they accepted my story that I was working as a film extra. Pauline and her husband were good people, and offered me real friendship. I think perhaps he never realised how I lived, but Pauline—she died some years ago—was most concerned for me. She often had me back to Ireland to stay with them for a rest—they had a large house and a happy one with two adopted children, a boy and a girl, since they could have none of their own. She passed me on good clothes and listened to me and offered me good advice—at times she would wipe the floor with me over my behaviour! I think she felt the rest of the family had given me a very raw deal, and that in some way it was up to her to make amends. I know she never stopped praying for me, and perhaps it is through her that I am where I am today: she would be very happy that I have stayed here so long.

There were people, however, who genuinely cared for prostitutes in the West End and in their way tried to do something to help: the Legion of Mary patrolled the same streets as we did. They were a band of Catholic women I first came across on a cold November evening in Shepherd Market. Two of these good ladies appeared out of the shadows and asked me in a very friendly way if I would like to go as their guest into a nearby café for a warm cup of coffee. As I wanted to get on with my work—I needed the money just then for the high rent of my flat—I declined, but I did take the card they offered me with their address on it. I got to know them quite well, and often in an evening would call in at their small office, which was then in Manchester Street. I was grateful for the offered cup of tea and the friendly conversation.

They were always trying to persuade me away from the sinful life I was living, however, and at times, if I saw them coming, I would dodge into a doorway to avoid their talk. I am sure they were good women with the very best intentions, and they did this work on a voluntary basis on top of a full-time job by day, but I feel they did not approach people like me in the right way. I feel they lacked the training and experience and organisation to deal with us. To begin with, like the policewomen, they were always in pairs, and they *would* approach us when we were on the job. Most of them were Irish—so for that matter were many of the prostitutes, and many of *them* had come, like myself, from good Catholic families. I got the impression that these good ladies had themselves lived very sheltered lives for the most part—many were from the country—and you could not expect them to understand and cope with the girls in the West End, some of whom were quite well educated, and in the racket only because a gay life of luxury appealed to them.

At times, through the Legion of Mary, I made some effort to get out, but each time it was disastrous. Once, a few days after I had had an abortion, I was feeling ill and depressed and was wondering what to do, when I thought of contacting them. They were delighted, and arranged for me to go down to a convent in the country which specially catered for girls like me — I found out when I got there, however, that their girls were much younger and for the most part on probation from the Courts. Two of the Legion took me down themselves on the following day, a Saturday, by train. I felt terribly ill — I did not realise it, but the abortion had not been complete, and the right place for me just then would have been hospital. The Legion had explained to the convent when they rang up that I was not well, and that they would be grateful if I could have a room on my own, instead of being in a large dormitory.

The Sisters gave me a room overlooking a large forest. Often in the early morning when I could not sleep I would sit quiet as a mouse in the dark by the wide open window, smoking a cigarette, while the scent of trees and flowers was fresh on the cold air. During the day, you could see the squirrels run up and down the tree trunks and along the boughs. I loved the peace of that room — when I could get to it! I felt the need of peace so badly.

The very next morning after my arrival I was told I would have to work in the laundry. (They took in a lot of outside work from the nearby towns.) I was quite willing to try anything once, although I felt awful and wanted nothing as much as my bed. My hours each day were from eight-thirty to five-thirty, with a short break for lunch and tea, and all that time I was standing. The first day, a large basket of handkerchiefs was dumped beside me and I set to work to iron them, but at the end of the afternoon, when the sister came along to see how much I had got through, I had only managed a dozen. I was roundly told off, and indeed, I felt ashamed myself that I had done so little, but the steam iron was so large and heavy for my small hands, and I was so tired and sick — there seemed no one to bother about the state I was in.

I felt the staff were pulling against me all the time I was

there. They did not like me smoking—I was the only girl who stuck out and insisted on being allowed to have a cigarette from time to time, though many were dying for a smoke. We had to keep silence in the laundry itself—not a word was allowed, and the sister-in-charge was always telling me off for singing over my work. I couldn't help it. At heart I am a happy sort of person and the tunes just burst out of me.

When the day's work in the laundry was over, and we had had supper, I would have liked to go to my room and my bed, but that was not allowed. Instead, we had to go into a sort of hall for recreation such as dancing—dancing with the other girls! (It was the last form of exercise I should have been taking at the time anyway.) My style of dancing did not meet with the approval of the sister-in-charge either: it was too modern for her liking, so I was forbidden to dance with those partners who aided and abetted me. And we prayed so much! Prayer is excellent in its place, but *that* was not it. Such an institution was just not fitted to deal with girls like me—it aimed to punish, not rehabilitate —I don't think that is the way to deal with anyone.

Two or three days after I arrived, I collapsed by my handker-chiefs. I had earlier suggested I might be allowed a chair, so that I could iron sitting down, and the sister had refused. I was given a day—only one—in bed. The following day I got up and went back to work, but a clash was inevitable. I had a terrific row with the sister-in-charge and at ten o'clock at night, they called a taxi for me—it took a good deal of the thirty shillings which was all I had in my purse—and I was dumped with my heavy luggage at the station to find my way back to London.

Waterloo was dreary and depressing when I arrived, and I had nowhere to go. I took a chance, and went by taxi to a hotel, where I explained to the receptionist that I could not pay for a room until I had been to the Post Office to draw some money. She sent for the manager, who at first was very reluctant to let me stay, but when I told him about my luggage, he relented.

I wonder what would have happened if I had not been lucky enough to have savings sufficient to pay there? The sisters never enquired how I would manage, they were so glad to see the back of me. Next morning, I rang up my two friends from the Legion of Mary. They were very upset that things had worked out so badly, but they did not want me to come back to London, and indeed, I had no wish to be back there myself. They pleaded with me to give the convent another try, and after a long struggle, I gave way and agreed.

My friends got in touch with the convent and arranged for me to return, but the sisters pointed out that I must be prepared to be treated exactly like the other girls. Foolishly, I agreed. I travelled down this time by myself. I felt so glad to be going back—I made myself feel as if I were going home: it was a wonderful thought. Alas, my reception was anything but home-like.

I was greeted with the fact that I must now change into the uniform the other girls were wearing and I would sleep in a dormitory. Smoking was absolutely forbidden, and all my belongings were to be taken away from me and stored while I was there. It was altogether too much—that was the end of that effort to get onto the right path. I was back in London the very same evening.

One raw, winter Saturday evening, I had been strolling round the Mayfair streets, feeling rather miserable—there were very few people about because of the cold, and business was bad. It was just after the passing of the Street Offences Act and two policemen had been keeping a close eye on me all evening. I did not want to go to a club or public house, so I kept on walking aimlessly, till I found myself passing the Roman Catholic church in Farm Street once more. On an impulse, I went inside. It was warm and friendly, and I sat down and began, almost without knowing it, to pray.

All the time that I was on the racket, as I said before, I could not receive the Sacraments of the Church, because I was living in sin and had no intention of making any effort to stop, but I felt their loss deeply. Often, when I slipped in at the back of a church—not only my own Roman Catholic ones, but those of other denominations—I would come out wishing I had the strength to break away from my life.

This evening I sat longer than usual—I did not want to leave the warmth and silence for the cold streets outside. The minutes ticked by. A few people started to come into the church and queue up for confession. I saw one or two priests go into their confessional boxes and I looked at them and I thought, 'Oh, God! If they only knew how I feel about my way of life at present. If only they could do something to help me!'

I could not help myself—I needed the help of someone else.

I went on sitting and by now all the people had been to confession. I sat there in envy of them and wondered just what sort of lives they led. The priests stayed on in the confessionals to see if anyone else was coming in. Then suddenly I could stand it no longer. I stood up from my seat, walked over and opened the door to one of the boxes. At the time, it seemed to me the nicest confessional I had ever stepped into, even all those years ago when I used to go to confession.

At this moment, the grille opened and I knew that the priest was waiting for me to start my confession, in the name of Christ.

'Father,' I said, 'I don't want to make my confession—I just want to talk to you.' Talk to him I did and told him my problems, and he talked to me so kindly. He kept calling me his poor child, and the tears were rolling down my cheeks. It was he who arranged with my Legion of Mary friends that I should try another convent. As I was about to leave the confessional, he asked me if I was in need of money, for if I was, he would go straight to his superior and ask him for some—that was not at that time a difficulty, however. When I got outside that church and back into the streets of Mayfair, I felt like running back inside and taking refuge there, so much did I hate my life at that time.

The convent to which I now went was a fee-paying one for women with all kinds of different problems, for the most part drugs and drink. I loved it there and stayed for over a year. I paid seven pounds a week, from my savings and by the help of a kind friend—this left me with barely enough for my cigarettes, let alone anything else, so money was a constant worry. Even though we paid, we were expected to do a lot of housework.

This convent was in a most beautiful part of the country, a sheep-farming district—and how I adored the new-born lambs! The sisters, unfortunately, were the same Order as those in the previous convent. I got the impression that they had very little interest in my welfare. They obviously had only a short-term stay in view, whereas I was looking for a place which would care for me for a very long time. The sisters, more-over, knew that I was a prostitute and they could not help treating me with distaste. They and the women who came as patients were such a very snobbish lot, although some of the women has as little to be snobbish about as I had.

I well remember one day when the sister-in-charge passed

me in the corridor and I noticed she was wearing a new pair of shoes. In a friendly way, I remarked how nice they were: she wiped the floor with me – I had no right to be so personal where someone of religion was concerned, she said. (I cannot help contrasting her with my dear Mother Oliver in the convent here. The other day, as Chippy and I came in from our walk, we met her looking very clean and neat in a new habit – most of the habits have been carefully patched and darned for years. I remarked how nice it looked: she thanked me with a delighted smile and said it was not often she received compliments – it made her feel really good.)

It was at that second convent that I had a very odd experience with an older woman which rather shook me. She had been married and had lived abroad a lot. She was clever and intelligent and about my own age. She dressed in a somewhat severe style, and always in slacks, excepts on Sundays. She was not particularly beautiful, but something about her attracted me from the first.

One morning I was sitting in my room stitching at a teacloth for one of my friends, when this girl knocked at my door. She said she had been asked by the sisters to go on an urgent errand to collect a lady from the station and could not finish cleaning out her room – would I be kind enough to do it for her?

From that day, my whole time was spent in caring for her and looking after her needs. I brought her her early morning cup of tea, made her bed, tidied her clothes – they were scattered all over the room so that it was difficult sometimes to know where to begin. I cleaned her many pairs of shoes and washed her panties. She, for her part, worked quite hard for the convent – she could drive and look after cars, decorate, weed the lawns, and goodness knows what else.

I believed everything she told me. The other patients warned me against her, but how was I to know that she was a terrible liar? For make no mistake, she was still heavily on drugs – she managed to get them from somewhere, over and above the official daily quota. Either the sisters did not know, or they turned a blind eye to it. On top of that, she smoked about forty cigarettes a day.

She worked so hard in the daytime that she retired to bed soon after tea. I would find her sitting up in bed reading after her bath. She was heavily under the influence of tablets and I suppose it was that and the relaxation which made her begin to act sexy. She told me she loved me and would stand by me from then on for life—and I, like a bloody fool, believed it all. I found her very attractive and appealing at first. Perhaps it was a natural reaction from a girl like myself who had spent so much time in the company of men and was so tired of them. Even then, I would never have made any further move—I was far too shy—until, one late spring morning, she kissed me passionately. I was very taken aback, although by then I so much wanted it. Our friendship went from strength to strength; there is no need to go into details, for it is a thing of the past I want very much to erase from my mind. The mental and physical strain of such an affair on both of us was terrific. I found no satisfaction in this carry-on—it got us nowhere, and I felt like a wet rag.

This affair lasted four or five months of my stay at the convent. When she went away for a week's holiday, I would receive passionate love letters from her each day. I used to be terrified the sister-in-charge would open one: in a way now, I am sorry she did not, as she would surely have seen where the blame rested. As it was, she crept into the room one day and found us both in a compromising situation. It was a shocking moment for me. I felt so ashamed of myself and so guilty. I got up and excused myself and just walked out of the room.

From that moment, it was obvious one of us must go and it was not likely to be her—she was far more useful than me. They threw me out and sent me back to London, which was just where I did *not* want to be. I cried with disappointment.

XII

THOUGH these attempts to break away failed, I had gradually been gathering friends around me who were interested in me, to all of whom I shall never cease to be grateful, for they all in their ways helped me on towards my present life, even if the particular solutions they offered did not work out at the time.

There was the good friend I met through offering to help address envelopes for Westminster Cathedral's appeal fund for completing its building. She was the Cathedral Administrator's secretary, and she was showing the volunteers what to do. I used to go in to help several mornings in the week, and one day, out of the blue, she asked me if I would like to go up to her flat for a cup of coffee some time – she said she was in most evenings. I went, and that was the start of a friendship which still exists. When I left the second convent, it was on a day she had come to visit me there. She took me back to London with her, and invited me to stay in her home for the time being.

I don't think she ever knew why, after six happy weeks there looking after the flat while she was at work and doing some of the cooking, which I found great fun, I suddenly announced I was leaving. Close by was the place where the Black Marias stopped on their way from the prisons to the Courts, to divide out their prisoners according to their destinations. This spot held a terrible fascination for me, and I could not keep away. The thought of the human tragedies behind the black forbidding windows of those vans preyed on my mind until it became more than I could bear, and I felt I must get right away from that part of London.

Father Hollings had left Westminster Cathedral by now for the Catholic Chaplaincy to the University of Oxford, and I did not know who to turn to at this time, for I felt I could not keep asking the same people over and over again. I had heard of a Father William Kahle at the Cathedral who was particularly interested in helping girls like me so one day when no one was waiting for him, I went over to his confessional and asked if I could speak with him. He came out and we sat down and I told him all about my problems. He went straight away and telephoned several religious houses to see if they would take me. He found one and drove me all the long way there himself in his battered old car — I was worried at what it must have cost him in petrol.

Alas, it was a very small convent, very closed in, and though I stuck it a few months, it was not the solution for me, with my love of being out of doors and unconfined, so I left once more.

Father Kahle is now a chaplain at Holloway and I can think of no one I would rather have to help me if ever I were sent to prison. He has had his own share of troubles, for his family was German and suffered at the hands of the Nazis. He is a saint of a man and makes me think of Father Pierre, the priest who works among down-and-outs in Paris. He has had a lot to do with running a house down in Kent for unmarried homeless mothers, another terribly important need.

The friend who will always have my deepest affection I first met a long time ago, quite by chance. He was visiting the Legion of Mary office where I had gone, as I sometimes did, for a cup of coffee and a chat — I was feeling tired and depressed, and it was somewhere I could go and get things off my chest. This quiet, rather vague, slightly-built man was asking them all about their work and how successful it was, and about the girls and the clubs — to my mind, their answers weren't as well-informed as they might have been. I asked who he was, and one of them told me he was Lord Pakenham (Lord Longford as he is now). A friend from the Home Office was taking him round to collect material for the debate he was about to introduce on the 1957 Wolfenden Report in the House of Lords.

As they passed me on their way out, I asked on an impulse if he would like to go with me and meet some of my friends. He seemed pleased and suggested I should get into the friend's car and direct them. I soon found out how deceptive the vague manner was — he was keenly interested in all I could tell and show him. First we drove through Hyde Park and he was most surprised when I pointed out the couples standing in the shadows there. Then we went along Curzon Street and to Shepherd Market, where I introduced him to the girls, and they were quite as tickled to talk to him as he was to meet them. When he asked one French girl who was a trained seamstress why she didn't come off the life and get herself a job, however, she retorted, 'Why should I, when I can earn £100 a week where I am!'

During my quite long stay at the second convent, I wrote to Lord Longford, because I knew he would be pleased to hear I was making the effort to get out of the old life at last. He immediately wrote back, inviting me over to his home to meet himself and his wife. Since then, he has shown himself a real friend at every turn, a father by adoption in fact, for I feel he shows me the love and respect usually reserved for a true daughter, and both he and his wife have written to me frequently. He invites me to lunch with him too at regular intervals, and several times this has been at the House of Lords. That was absolutely wonderful. The food was very English, but extremely well-cooked. Everyone was so courteous—his secretary and I were treated almost as if we were members of the House ourselves! And I was introduced to all sorts of really famous people — it was so exciting. For this, but much more for the kindness he has shown me in so many ways over the years, it is a friendship I shall always treasure.

At present, he is running the New Horizon centre in Soho, where social misfits such as drug addicts, or youngsters who have left home or been pushed out of their lodgings or left Borstal, can go during the day to have a cup of coffee, or go to sleep (because most of them walk the streets during the night) or just have a chat. I have been there several times and each time I am staggered afresh at the hard work put in by Lord Longford and his helpers.

The boy who is the club leader was sacked from the Hornsey College of Art during the student troubles there, and went off to learn social work from someone working with youngsters like the Soho lot. Then he came to help at the centre. He is very good with them all, because he dresses like them and talks their language—even their bad language! Then there is a girl always on duty who used to be Lord Longford's secretary. She had no previous experience with this work, but she has a great love of people and that goes for a lot. Other people go in to help from time to time, like the girl who was secretary to Lord Longford when I first met him. She is the dearest sweetest person one could wish to meet, so sympathetic and understanding.

She has a regular job in the Treasury as well, but works in her spare time at the centre, and everyone finds her easy to talk to.

When I arrived there last, there were about eight or nine drug addicts in the club. They all seemed to be relieved that for a few hours at least, they had some form of shelter and relaxation. The room they were lounging in was homely and comfortable with bright posters on the walls. For those who needed it, there was a cup of good strong coffee, all for free. The leader had provided paper, brushes and oils for those who wanted to paint—that was what most of them seemed to be doing but some were tapping on typewriters. In the place of honour on the wall of my little room in the convent hangs a country scene one of them painted that day specially for me. They were the nicest bunch of teenagers one would wish to meet, although drifters and dossers and all on the road to ruin—a very short road for some of them.

Here in this club, however, started by Lord Longford because as a Christian he felt he could not stand by and see these young-sters go to waste without trying to do something for them, they find a helping hand. No questions are asked, no 'Don't do this!' or 'Don't do that!' They don't have to have a problem or a reason to go there, but someone is always sitting waiting if they want advice. The only thing they all have in common is that they are young—they come from all sorts of backgrounds, yet I have never seen any friction there among the different personalities and types of problem, and the workers say the same thing. They are helping the youngsters to *want* help—when they see themselves accepted by ordinary people it makes some of them at least want to do something about themselves.

Three-quarters of them have tried drugs, though not all of them have stayed on them. They are always keen to help each other to come off. One girl's boy friend was keeping her on drugs, then he went away for a while. A group of them kept her talking one night until the centre where she got her supplies closed. (Someone had a supply in her pocket in case the girl became desperate.) They got her a long way along the path to recovery, but unluckily, the boy friend returned and she was back where she started.

That day I last visited the club, I asked Lord Longford when he thought of retiring from all the social work in which he is involved (he also spends a lot of time helping long-term prisoners). He said he *wasn't* thinking of it—he expected he would carry on until he dropped. The world of suffering misfits will indeed be a very sad place then, without the bond of friendship which exists between himself and us.

Another friend I must now mention is Father Joe Williamson, who runs two escape houses where girls like I once was can go when they feel the desire to break away from their life, and he has just started a third in Birmingham. Father Joe is an Anglican: I first came across him one Sunday afternoon when I had squatted down on the floor of my small flat in Kensington to read the newspapers. In the *Empire News*, there was an article on Father Joe and his house in Wellclose Square, Stepney, which offered a helping hand to prostitutes. I was so moved by what I read that I sat straight down and wrote to him, telling him what I was and how much I admired the work he was doing.

A letter came back by return, inviting me to go along and have tea on a Sunday afternoon with Father Joe and his wife. I not only had my tea with them but supper too, the first of many, many visits and happy meals and talks there. They lived in a Stepney vicarage, and it was the very first time I had ever penetrated the heart of the East End. What I saw there really appalled me. As I walked along Leman Street and Cable Street, I could see nothing but vice, open and unashamed vice, and the smell of dirt and degradation was terrible. Juke-box music blared out through the doors of pubs and filthy cafés, and girls in their early teens, lovely-looking girls but old before their time, were trying to attract men passing by. My heart felt sad for them: here was I, an older person, of the selfsame profession, and I knew, as they did not, the heartbreaks and pitfalls they would come across later if they went on in the same way.

As I walked towards the vicarage, I felt quite nervous of the seedy characters I saw all round me. A large car driven by a well-dressed businessman cruised slowly past me, trying to pick me up. Some of the thugs lounging in the doorways of the empty boarded-up houses had old scars of razor-fights across their cheeks, and they smelt disgustingly. Many of the loiterers were coloured, for this was near enough to the docks to attract all the West Indians who are too unstable to keep their jobs there. The thought struck me that my life in the West End was heaven compared to this. I would rather starve than find myself at this lowest level of existence. I had often thought how vicious Soho was, but when I came to know Stepney, there was no comparison.

I was heartily welcomed by Father Joe and his wife. What struck me most about both them and their home was the warmth and kindliness. They oozed out welcome and love, though Father Joe could be very straightforward and down to earth and did not mince his words when necessary. The meal Mrs. Williamson had prepared was delicious: good, wholesome food, and it tasted wonderful to someone like myself who had lived for years more or less out of a tin.

We must have been talking – straight, honest-to-God talking, for that is the sort of people they both are – for some two hours, when Father Joe at last took me over to see the Wellclose Square house. He introduced me to some of his staff and I found the same kindness, understanding and charity in all of them. I often dropped in at weekends after that, and I was never at any time made to feel an outcast because of my profession. I was made so welcome that first Sunday that when the time came for me to say goodnight and return to my own haunts, even though my flat was Buckingham Palace compared to the hovels of the East End, I felt sad that the visit was over and I had to go.

At that time, I had no intention of giving up my way of life, even though the Williamsons had tried to make me see sense, but I looked at things very differently some months later, when not long after I left the second convent and the friend's flat near Westminster Cathedral, I was attacked, as I told you, by one of my customers and was lucky to escape with my life. I went to Father Joe in great distress and he kindly offered me a little room in the Wellclose Square house until we could make plans for me to get away from it all.

One day, the cook-helper failed to turn up, because she was ill. They asked me if I would take over, and I was very much taken aback, as I had seldom cooked anything larger than an egg in my life. There was no one else, however, so I said I would, and duly reached for the cookery book. Forgive me if I sound swollen-headed, but I turned out some terrific meals! Everything I cooked was eaten with relish. Mostly we were about fourteen at table, so it was quite a job. Father Joe insisted on paying me pocket money for doing this, and I was delighted.

Much and all as I liked everyone connected with the house, however, I could not have stayed there long. It was in such terrible surroundings, and I wanted to get right away from the sordidness of big cities, the noise of the traffic, the temptations.

Besides, the other girls were much younger than me and very immature. It was such a clean, home-from-home place, though. Every comfort was provided for those who passed through. I remember the smiling faces and the affection of the staff, the spotless bed-linen, the hot water in the clean bath, the food — plain, but manna to a worn-out, undernourished body — the glowing fire, the warm glass of milk before snuggling down into a bed all one's very own — a bed of my own has always meant such a lot to me.

I wish that there could be escape houses like this for girls to go to if they wanted, not just in the East End, but in each district, and certainly some right in the country, as Father Joe's are not. It would be no good having just one central house, however, mixing many different types and ages under one roof: it would never work. There would have to be several, for like every other type of people, prostitutes are of many different classes and personalities. In these escape houses it ought to be possible for them to have a small bed-sitting room of their very own, paying only a low rent — it would be a long time before they were strong and stable enough to manage an ordinary, sufficiently well-paid job.

It was through Father Joe that I did, in fact, take an ordinary outside job for a while, living in his hostel out of London, at Goodmayes near Ilford. I worked as a cleaner on British Railways. I kept at it for about six weeks and loved it: the other women were marvellous — really the salt of the earth, though they took some time accepting me: they thought I was a snob, and enjoyed coming out with some crude four-letter word to shock me — until they learnt that I was very much one of themselves! I enjoyed the work too — it felt really useful: I cleaned the trains at the main depot, brushing and Hoovering the upholstery, scrubbing the floors, ceilings and panelwork, cleaning out the very dirty lavatories and polishing up the brass handles of each compartment. We worked in shifts and the money was wonderful for those days: some weeks it was as much as eleven pounds. The night shift was tiring, however: I found it difficult to make up the lost sleep by day. Even on the racket, I had always finished by 2.00 a.m. at the latest, and whenever I wanted to I could take off the odd hour for a quick nap. I left in the end because I failed an eye test in my medical, and the others were as sorry as I was when I went. I could never have done an office type of job, where I was confined to my seat for the same hours each day. Nothing has suited me as well as my present work, with its variety and the freedom of being out of doors so much.

I was fed up at losing my job, but I was also getting rather fed up with the surburban pettiness of the neighbourhood. I became so depressed, I began to be afraid I would have a nervous breakdown and would have to go into hospital. Suddenly I packed up all my clothes, rang for a taxi and told the woman in charge I was going. I went down to Sussex: I had been there on day trips, and I felt a holiday by the sea was just what I needed at that time.

The Goodmayes house itself was a beautiful place if it had not been so towney. I was one of the very first girls to go there — I remember thinking that the lovely fitted carpets, the soft blankets and pretty bedspreads, the bright clean bathrooms, and the charming garden with the goldfish pond, were almost too good to last. I wonder how later visitors have treated them.

The sad thing was that even there, of all places, there was a social barrier between the girls and the helpers. Quite a number of these were young men, but there was a definite understanding that they were not allowed to fall in love because you were 'outside', and friendships were not encouraged. It seemed the more pity because some of them were just the sort of people I would have liked to marry!

I am still very much in contact with Father Joe: he never forgets to write on my birthday, at Christmas or at Easter, and now he has retired from active work in the houses, I have often been down to his home in Sussex, to stay with the Williamsons — I treasure the memory of trudging along the seashore with Father Joe and an old perambulator, in which we stacked pieces of driftwood from the beach for the evening fires. After years of city life, the calm and ordinariness of life with the Williamsons is balm. I love to sit in their large window which faces the sea and watch through binoculars the large liners passing far out, on their way into Southampton. One thing I must say — although Father Joe belongs to a different church, the Church of England, he has never once tried to persuade me to leave my own for his: on the contrary, when I was keeping out of religion's way he worked hard to make me contact priests of my own church, or the Legion of Mary again. It was through him, in fact, that I first heard of Father Kahle, who had often been down to the East End, to the house in Wellclose Square, because he was himself interested in helping girls to escape from the streets.

While I was seeking round for some way to get out of my old life, it was another account in the Sunday papers which once more led me to try out another venture to help social misfits in London and elsewhere—the Simon Community. I wrote and told Lord Longford of the article I had read, and asked if he could help me in contacting the man who was running the Community, Anton—I forget his other name. The meeting was arranged, and I liked Anton, and what I heard and saw of his work—his flat at St. Leonards-on-Sea held, besides himself and his mother, five of the 'misfits', all male. We drank coffee and smoked cigarettes and talked a lot, and it was arranged that I should have a sort of staff job, at a pound a week, at the farmhouse in the country that the Community had just bought.

It was an absolute haven of peace to me: it seemed just what I had most longed for, even though the architecture and the state of repair were nothing to write home about. We had wonderful food—Eric, who was an alcoholic, was also the most splendid cook. As the only woman there, I had a small—very, very small—room to myself; the rest all had to share. There were Anton himself, Eric, Shawn (who was in charge of money matters and drove Anton round on his many missions), and about four others. One of them saw to all Anton's correspondence and typing.

I found myself spending most of my time doing the housework, although I did not like being confined indoors. I could not bear to live in squalor—not that this house was ever what you could call squalid—so I did the washing-up, cleaned the kitchen and dining room and laid the tables for meals, made beds and cleaned the bedrooms—and the bathrooms: the baths were the hardest of all, with men working on the land, and nearly always there was a flood of water on the floor to be mopped up.

In what time remained, I was out on the smallholding. One day, Anton announced he was going to buy some pigs, so I started to clean out the sties, which had not been used for years, in readiness. I swept away all the mud and dung left from the last inhabitants, then I went down on my hands and knees and scrubbed the whole building out with soap, hot water and disinfectant. I was proud of my work—all that was needed now was the litter: I was looking forward to watching them fatten up under my care.

They came all right—and I went! When it became obvious that Anton was going to be late home, I went off to bed. He evidently arrived in his van with the pigs in the early hours of the morning. A little later, I woke up feeling thirsty, put on my dressing gown to go to the bathroom, when I heard a strange noise coming from the kitchen. I went down to investigate, and there were the piglets, four of them, squeaking and grunting and rushing all over the floor, which was in a shocking state. The smell was awful: I could have wept when I saw just where Anton had dumped them, when he could so easily have taken them out to the sty. At this moment, Anton himself came into the kitchen and I just let rip.

The very next day, when Anton was out somewhere, I ran away from the farm, taking with me a little dog which had been left in his care. It was a very nervous animal and had become very attached to me—I gave it all the love and care I could. It was very much of a town dog and hated the countryside. Every night while I was at the farm, this dog slept across the end of my bed, and I could not bear the thought of leaving it behind.

I intended to return to London and find a bed-sitting room there—it would have been rather difficult with a dog, but I did not stop to think of that. I caught the train, but at a big stop along the line, we waited for over fifteen minutes and I suddenly decided to get off there. After a lot of searching, I found a room with a very odd landlady, a Roman Catholic of about fifty, just recently married, who laboured under the delusion that her husband was St. Joseph and she was the Virgin Mary; she kept assuring me their marriage was pure and virginal. The dog and I were there for three weeks—it was a most unhappy time. I spent the days trudging round trying to find a convent to take me in, the landlady's moods were uncertain, the dog fretted if I left it even for a little while, and I had very little money for the two of us. After some time, I telephoned the Simon Community and eventually they collected the dog from me. I should never have taken it without permission, but it seemed so unhappy, and was so attached to me.

The Simon Community was not for me, although all the time I was there with that group of men, who came from all walks and stations of life, I was very happy, and not one of them made any kind of immoral advance to me—or, for that matter, I to them. I was sincerely sorry that it did not work out—the freedom of their outdoor life had great attractions, but I must have some sort of order and discipline in my life, and with their set-up you never knew where you were. Anton and his gang were too swinging for me: at a certain point, I become rather a conservative. I have insufficient patience to cope with alcoholics and drug addicts, although I am pretty tolerant of other people's failings.

I still did not want to go back to London and I was far from well, so I took a flat in Sussex. I was getting sickness benefit—about three pounds ten a week. The rent was two pounds fifteen which left me very little for food and cigarettes, particularly as the gas fire and stove ate sixpences. I had some small savings, but I did not dare break into those—I had learnt at last always to keep something for emergencies. So I ate chiefly bread and marg., jam and eggs, and when the weather was cold and one of the walls ran with damp, I sat shivering and miserable rather than part with one precious sixpence for the fire.

In fine weather, I wandered along the seafront, and sometimes found a man who would take me out for a meal and perhaps for a drive to some secluded spot. My landlady was much too watchful for me ever to take anyone back to my flat and the police at this time, after the passing of the Street Offences Act, were very vigilant for girls soliciting. I was ashamed at the smallness of the money presents I now received, but even those made all the difference to my food situation.

When life over the years had become too much of a strain, I used to go over to Dublin for a while to a private nursing-home run by a doctor friend of our family, for a rest. I had been saving up for this the time I had to bail out Beryl. Now this doctor wrote to ask if I would go and live there, free of charge, in return for some help in the patients' dining room. It was nearly Christmas, and it sounded a good idea, as I was not looking forward to spending that season on my own. I stayed only five months. It was no good—they *would* try to make me fit in with *their* idea of what was right and proper. They tried to stifle the real me—and I am far too old to change now.

Back I went to Sussex. I found a very small attic flat in a rather shady place, a pair of old houses converted into about twenty little flatlets. I was scared stiff of getting involved in trouble, and the flat was filthy too: I can't think how I ever came to take it. The rent was two pounds ten a week, and I was back on sickness benefit, so somehow I had to get some money.

The chatting-up of men and the petting had lost their attraction for me — I suppose I was getting older — and I made up my mind to find a job, though while I was receiving assistance, this was against the law. I washed up in a restaurant two or three days a week, and scrubbed down the kitchen floor. For this, I received the wonderful sum of a pound a day. The owners said I was a good worker, and so I was. I began at eight-thirty in the morning and went on till six — it was hard work, and the pace was very fast. By the end of a day I was so exhausted, I made steps straight for bed. This job did not last long either — I could not stand the loud clatter of plates or being confined indoors. The owners tried to persuade me to stay, but I had to be able to get outside as well, and not be confined indoors all the time.

Now I had nothing to do all day again. I took to going to the local Courts and following the cases, but it was very sordid. There were some really vicious people about, worse than in Soho, though Sussex as a county was all right. Suddenly, I did not want any more of it. I had heard or read, sometime, somewhere, about my present convent. I went to a telephone box and put in a long-distance call to Reverend Mother — it was Mother Oliver in those days, so now you see why she is so very dear to me. I asked her if she would take me, on any terms that she liked. At that time, by great good luck (or something more!) she wanted someone in the convent kitchen to help Sister Margaret, who was not very well, so she suggested I might like the job. I willingly accepted and asked her when I could begin. She said she would write to me in a few days' time, when she had thought the matter over. That was not good enough for me: I told her I wanted to come to the convent that very day — I felt I must get away to safety and to someone kind. Reverend Mother said that at that moment, she had no room empty: I begged her to let me camp down in a coal cellar — anywhere, if only she would let me come.

That settled it. She agreed, and I took a taxi, piled with my bits and pieces, all the long distance to the convent — the fare of it very nearly broke me. The Sisters must have been amazed at the sight and I am quite sure they wondered what on earth they had let themselves in for.

I went to work in the kitchen, but I did not like it: it was far too confined a job for me. I had many rows with the kitchen sister, and each and every day that I spent there, I debated whether or not I should pack up and leave—and each and every day, I expected Reverend Mother to tell me to go. Then an idea occurred to me: I would ask to work outside, on the estate, and from that day I have never looked back.

Reverend Mother once told me they will never ask me or force me to leave the shelter of this convent—I think it would kill me now if I had to go. More than anything I have ever known in my life before it is my real home. If only other religious houses would extend the hand of friendship and Christianity to someone like myself—I do not suggest they should take a number of us; just one girl in each convent—and treat her just as I have been treated during these last three years, as one of themselves and a child of Christ. The peace, the regular daily routine, the discipline, and above all the love and affection are what I would not find in any ordinary job. I am not normal, I know—how could I be, after so long a time living such an abnormal life? The past is always with me: not a very pretty picture to remember for the rest of my life. I can think of no one who could have shown more tolerance and allowance for me than the Community who have taken me into their care.

Epilogue

IT IS early morning again. I must have been up since half past three and the milkman came long ago. It is nearly time to walk Chippy out before Mass — I still have to do that. A week ago, Mother Oliver decided Chippy's season was over. Yesterday, however, when we went over the fields in the afternoon, dogs appeared from every corner like magic and I had an awful job to get her home again. I think all of us here are rather ignorant about Chippy's sex life!

. . .

There was fog again this morning and it was even quieter than usual out of doors. The occasional sound of a distant car was very eerie. It was reassuring to hear the Angelus bell ring out from the convent chapel, though it had a queer sharp note instead of its usual echoing ring. When I got back, the postman was sitting in the hall with the pot of hot tea and plate of bread and butter the sisters give him each morning.

. . .

We have come out of Mass. Sometimes I ask myself if I am not some sort of damned hypocrite, but in my heart of hearts, I know it is not so. There is a great deal to atone for in my past, and this is my way of doing it. The Mass has become the highlight of my day: that time when Christ gives Himself to us in the Blessed Sacrament lends some sort of meaning and unity to all the ups and downs of ordinary daily life. I've only missed Mass one morning since I came here, and a very empty and lost sort of day it felt afterwards.

I found Sister Margaret in the kitchen filling the breakfast teapots — I used to like it when she was in charge of the kitchen. She moves like a flash and everything is kept spotless. I looked forward to feastdays, because I knew she would bake such delicious cakes.

Reverend Mother has been in bed with a sore throat this week. It is not like her or any of the sisters to give in and go to bed unless they are really ill. While I was up in the village, I went into the greengrocer's and bought her a grapefruit, and Sister Margaret prepared it for me and put it on Mother's tray. From the report that came back of her delight at receiving it, you would have thought I had given her manna from heaven. Later, as I passed through the garden, a window was thrown open and a voice called my name. I looked up and saw just the head and shoulders of Reverend Mother, tightly wrapped in a blue dressing gown. She dropped me a note, and disappeared from view, saying she must not stay by the window. When I opened it in my room afterwards, I found a lovely letter of thanks for my 'generosity and thoughtfulness'.

Incidentally, Mother Angela has just got back from Rome, and to my great surprise, she brought me back a present—a gold chain with a medal of the present Pope, and St. Christopher on the other side. It is a beauty, a real beauty and I am so thrilled with it. I have had more little presents here than I ever received when I was in the outside world. If I wanted presents, I used to buy them for myself—but somehow, it feels much better to be given them by someone else after all!

Mother Angela is Principal of the old people's home. She is very tall, very slim and very lively, but don't ask me how old she is! Once, she was expecting her brother on a visit. I asked if he was married and she said no, so I asked his age and, with a twinkle, she replied he was in his nineties. She can't be so very much younger. We have most interesting conversations about everything under the sun, and I like her terrifically.

. . .

I spent the morning trying to light bonfires with the garden rubbish—there were the apple-tree prunings and some old branches, but it was just no good. The wind was blowing from the east for all it was worth, and they would burn up for a few minutes and then go out.

Sister Hilary and I had a fine time lopping off those branches from the trees which were darkening the windows. We sawed and chopped away, swinging out on the ropes, which kept breaking and sending one or other of us head over heels onto the soft earth. We had one very narrow escape—from the wrath of

Reverend Mother. One of the trees fell on the very side we were trying to avoid, and just missed the windows of the home. It took down some of the gutter as it was—I held my breath as it fell.

I have also been helping Sister Hilary prepare a room in the home for its new occupant. It is a lovely autumn day now, and the sunlight streamed in on the new paint and paper she has just decorated it with. We put down a wall-to-wall carpet, moved back the wardrobe and dressing table and made up the bed, then brought in the new owner's luggage all ready for her arrival.

The old ladies are so well looked after. Every birthday without fail is marked by an iced cake laden with fruit, with candles on top. At Christmas, Sister Hilary and Sister Ursula work like beavers, up on chairs or tables every second that can be spared from their duties, hanging up decorations, while I run from one place to another fetching and carrying for them. It looks so lovely on Christmas Eve when it is finished and the kitchens are full of Christmas fare. At the Midnight Mass, it struck me what a family we all were, the Community, the old people and the outside staff like myself. The chapel was packed—all the old people who could walk were there, and for the rest, the chaplain held another Mass during the day in the home.

During my time here I have seen many of the old people fall sick and die. When they are on the danger list, one of the religious sisters always sits up with them at night, even though the lay nurse is on duty. Even when they are too ill to be cared for in the home, a sister from the convent stays at their bedside in hospital day and night. They drop all other work to go, and these old ladies never feel alone at the last.

I was talking of Christmas. One regular event then is the little school party, with jellies, ice cream and games. This year, Sister Barbara asked me if I would dress up as Father Christmas, as she felt I knew the children and how to handle them. It was a rip-roaring success. I arrived at the school front door, then climbed into a child-size truck (lucky I'm so small!) with my sack on my back. There was a shout of delight when they saw me, though one or two little faces looked scared. My truck was drawn by four of the older boys into the playroom and I waved and bowed to them, calling out 'Merry Christmas! Merry Christmas!' in a gruff voice.

We began with a sing-song—all the Christmas songs and favourite nursery rhymes. I sang in a deep mannish voice to avoid giving myself away. Every child then had a small gift from my sack, and I told each of them I would be bringing something nice on Christmas Eve. Everyone seemed to be there, all the sisters, the chaplain and a great many of the children's mothers and old people.

This is my life now and these are its excitements. It seems to me that I have never been so happy and life has never been so full. I have changed a great deal. I used to do what I liked and take orders from no one. Now I do as I am asked, even if sometimes the old rebellious spirit rises a little at first. I have been here nearly four years, the longest period I have ever spent in one place in my whole life. For all that time, I have had nothing to do with sex and yet oddly enough I scarcely miss it.

And the future? How can I tell? I think I would like to live right in the country, not on the edge of a town, as we are here. The very sight of the countryside, the peace, the birds in the air, the farmyard animals, the trees, the wild life, seems to bring me closer and closer to the one from whom all life stems, God Almighty. Don't get me wrong. I am no saint—not by a long way: how could I be?—but in my heart of hearts I know the only way I shall ever be whole is to follow the path Christ wants me to take and no other. There are times when I ask myself if maybe I could undertake another kind of life, more cloistered, more disciplined and more religious. I doubt very much, however, if any religious organisation would accept me or if I would fit in with any of them.

I have another secret dream constantly with me, that one day I may find some way to go to the very wilds of Scotland and there stay and end my days. I would not mind living in some crofter's cottage—in fact, that is what I should love: to be able to go about dressed in my own bohemian way, no artificial conventions, my own natural self.

I want to get nearer to God, and I find I can do that best not in the noise and rush of the world but when I can see His divinity in nature. The present day unprincipled attitude to living, the permissive society, appals and horrifies me. I have not overnight become some sort of prude, but the emphasis nowadays on free sex for all seems to me very evil. Sex can be a wonderful thing, but it must be hallowed for our use by the bond and sacrament of marriage — I believe that, deep down, that has always been my view, in spite of what has gone before in my life. Sometimes, I think I would like to marry again, to have another chance to prove this.

But whatever the future holds, at least I am no longer afraid of it, for now I know it lies in God's hands.